WHEN THEY
WALK THROUG
THE DOOR

WHEN THEY WALK THROUGH THE DOOR

WILLIAM EVANS

Dedication

I dedicate this book to Sue, who has stood by me through all the good times, as well as the not so good times of my career. It is often said: behind any successful man, you will find a good woman.

We started this journey when I was a fitter and she supported me every step of the way.

Working long hours initially to make a living and becoming a workaholic has its downside for any relationship. We're still together today; she deserves a long service medal, obviously 'diamonds', darling.

Our children often had a missing Dad, so I am sorry for that. However, I did my best to give them all every opportunity in life. They, in return have provided eight super grandkids.

I hope in years to come they will read this book and discover a side of me that maybe they did not know or understand.

Love you all.

Acknowledgements

Daniel Priestley advocates that Key People of Influence should write a book. Well this sparked my imagination, and Covid gave me the time to think and finally decide to embark on this project.

With the idea firmly fixed in my head, my research into book writing convinced me to seek help. I called Gavin Ingham Brooke, a friend and PR colleague who I have worked with over the years both at Otis and D2E, and asked for his help. Being brave, Gavin said he would relish the opportunity to be involved. Gavin became the lead ghost writer.

We needed an outsider view of the book's messages. Fortune struck again and I met Maaike Van Renterghem who is an independent consultant, specialising in Emotional Intelligence. Maaike provided her angle to the key learning points.

Colour and imagination was added by the highly talented Maramgoni, a Brazilian commercial artist. His enthusiasm for this project was inspirational.

To all of my contributors, I am immensely grateful, thank you.

Do You Know What?

It is a warm summer's day, on the eve of a Bank Holiday weekend in a Pimlico mews house office, in the 2020s.

The man who is sitting at the desk has full grey hair, a sharp jacket and the time-worn face of experience. He wears a restless, inquisitive expression.

It's hard to tell his age: he could be in his mid-sixties. In common with one of his heroes, Mick Jagger, it seems he really doesn't do nostalgia.

The look is solid and engaging. He's serious, deadpan even, but with a hint of half-believing humour always ready to break through. It's as if he won't take anything at face value, even himself. He's able to reset on a sixpence.

On the day he is speaking, the world is dominated by new fears – of emerging AI, climate change, and inflation caused by a war raging in eastern Europe, even for an ailing Queen Elizabeth II – but the clear London voice ranges without hesitation over seven decades of an extraordinary life-journey.

It's a journey that has taken him from the streets of Tulse Hill to a global HQ in Farmington, Connecticut, Singapore, Japan and thence back to Brighton and Portugal; from oily rag to self-improving global businessman – and a doyen of vertical transportation.

William Louis Wood Evans was born on 17th September 1948. His father was Welsh, his mother came from Portsmouth.

He records the facts of his early life simply and calmly:

'When I was very young in the late fifties, I had two sisters that were much older than me, in fact 12 and 13 years older so, you know, when I turned 8, both of them had left home.

'One had already left when she was 18, when I was 6, so you know, so I'm pretty much a single child.

'I know my dad was joking, but he often used to say I was a mistake. Now, whether or not I began as an imposition to his life, I don't really know. I think he tried his best to be an involved father, but there was a huge age gap.

'Then, when I was 15, he decided to go and live in Wales on his own as he'd retired after being in poor health.

'So, my mum stayed behind in London to look after me until I was 20 years of age and then all of a sudden she let me know: "I'm going to live in Wales, and you're on your own."

'So, from the age of 20, here I am living on my own and, I'll be honest with you, I didn't have a clue, but I had to get a clue pretty bloody quick, if you know what I mean.

'A lot of people, especially people very close to me say to me now: "You're pretty much like your father, you're quite happy to live on your own" – but I'm not sure I want to put that too strongly in this book.

'But the thing is when I left Otis, the company I had spent over 35 years working for, I actually retired. After four months, I just couldn't stand it. I couldn't stand not doing anything and I think that in itself says something important about me.

'I really dread to think what I would do if I didn't work, you know what I mean, because, I mean, I love football. I'll be honest with you, I also love music, I mean, I really love The Rolling Stones. I see Mick Jagger as very important in my life purely because he's older than me and he's still rocking and I always say: all the time he's rocking, I'm rocking, you know.

'He's bloody amazing... Jesus Christ, I mean, these guys have had an amazing life and they're still alive... My personal life is very much embroiled in business life – pretty much like Roy Markham, whom we'll meet later in this book. Roy struggled to live his life without work you know, and I think maybe that's what I'm like.

'Well, you see, there are a lot of lessons learnt from those personal experiences.

'Take my own start in life: I was never, for instance, babysat by any of my grandparents. I do recall that my father and mother sent me, I don't know what the intention behind it was, but I had to go and stay with my grandmother. My grandfather got killed in the

First World War.

'So, there I was staying with my grandmother for a week or two, I don't know why, but obviously there was something going on for me to be there, and I remember the visit to her house, but I never remember her coming back to our house.

'Then, as for the other grandparents down in Portsmouth, I can remember going to visit them three or four times, maybe five times; my mum's parents, but they didn't act like grandparents do today. Take my wife, Sue, that's her true occupation: looking after our grandkids. It's so different today.

'So, fast forward, aged twenty, I was on my own and I had to earn money to live. I never had the chance to say: "Shit, I'm short, can you loan me some money this week?" Never never! You know, to save for a deposit for my first apartment I worked seven days a week for nearly seven years, you know, I worked weekends for a mate of mine. That's literally how it was.

'Whereas today, now, it is with so many families: "Can you loan me some money..." you know, all that sort of thing. I think that early hardship gives you resilience.

'Out of adversity, there is an opportunity. I'm always positive; I don't linger on history.

'Certainly in my early days at Otis, if I wasn't resilient there'd a been hell to pay!

'When I first started working there I worked with this guy, Jimmy Giles, who's in one of the chapters, I mean, he taught me a lot of positive stuff, but he also taught me a lot of negative stuff. He treated me like shit because it was a game to him.

'It wasn't that he treated me like shit because he was a spiteful person, he treated me like shit because he thought it was funny.

'And the only thing that kept me going through that... I mean, I just thought, "Oh my God, I don't know if I can put up with all of this" (and it did take me a long time) ...was my resilience. I'd left the security of a bank job and then I'd had three weeks on the dole, literally in the dole queue and I vowed to myself, this will never ever happen to me again, right.

'Okay, so the idea of the book was brought about purely because I was sitting around doing nothing during Covid. And a lot of people I work with often joke with me: "Oh, Bill, you're full of war stories, you ought to write a book about them all."

'I started to think, you know what, there's an awful lot of business books out there. It's like an ego-trip for a lot of people; they want to write a business book.

'In my case, I thought, you know what, I've come from a very humble background. I didn't go to university, I came out of my starting jobs at Barclays Bank and American Express, and I was lucky enough to get a job at Otis because I was told: "They take anybody." Then I rose through the ranks of Otis to, you know, the giddy heights of the company's World Headquarters in Farmington, Connecticut.

'But here's the thing, I rode my career path based upon picking up inputs from various people that actually gave me inspiration along the way. And whenever I looked at it, I thought to myself, you know, that person taught me this and that person taught me something else. I thought, why don't I just start writing down all these things?

'At the end of the day, I owe a lot of people. I owe a lot of my career progression to them. They are the ones who gave me the confidence to rise through the ranks and to start my own business – quite late in life, for that matter. And so now, I've got two companies and basically, I'm leaning on the experiences of the past. It's all down to certain individuals giving me inspiration in certain things.

'That was the initial thought behind this book.

'Then I wondered, well, who would want to read it anyway? And I started to realise that there's a whole bunch of people who are out there, similar to me, who haven't had the privilege of attending university or, for whatever reason, haven't had the benefit of a big formal education.

'So many people learn in totally different ways, I learnt that much during my time on the Otis University, when I was in my forties. Some people can pick things up easily by reading a book, others can see a film. Other people can learn on the job. I think I'm an on-the-job person.

'I thought if I could actually write all these things down, it's got to be in a way that people can learn it on the job, rather than the formal Harvard-style approach. Formal as in: "This is Michael Porter, da-de-da-de-da."

'I wanted my book to be in my own words and relived, if you like, in the present again, just as it happened to me. I want it to be almost as easy to read as *The Sun* newspaper, not *The Financial Times*. I want it to be as interesting as my life has been, as I have lived it. And then I thought, with all these people that I've come across in my career, what was the one thing they had that really stuck in my mind?

'I suppose, truthfully, what all these people all had was charisma. And charisma is all about something immediately noticeable about the person, that, when they walk through the door, you say: "Ah, I want to go and talk to that guy! Ah, I want to go and talk to him."

'They walk through the door and there's something about them. It doesn't mean to say that they're dressed in Savile Row, it means that there's something about them that exudes charisma. You know, we see and hear about a lot of the personalities today, from Boris Johnson to famous footballers and people like that. They've all got charisma. It is something that you can't really describe – charisma – but my definition of it is: when they walk through the door, I want to talk to 'em.

'So, what is it they've got that creates the charisma? Generally speaking, it's confidence. You know, they're confident about what they believe in, or confident about what they do, and so I started to think, well, do you know what, I could write a book around the characters I've met who've changed my life.

'I met, you know, Mr Wilson … who was Mr Wilson? Well, he was my first bank manager and he was the man that said: "Look, young man, if you can't afford a decent suit, make sure you wear a silk tie."

'Well, that reminds us you don't get a second chance to make a first impression. For me it flows from Mr Wilson saying you need a silk tie, but what does he really mean by that? It means a lot of things, like: you don't have to be expensively dressed, you don't have to have the best haircut, but the one thing you do have to understand is – and I repeat – you don't get a second chance to make a first impression. So, we can talk about how I started to include that idea in everything I do.

'You've got to recognise that you've got this opportunity all the time to sell yourself and if you don't realise you're a product, then, probably, you won't be that successful …

'So, I thought, yes! We can write a book about these people that walk through the door and about the main thought or theme associated with them. When I look back on them, there's so many things behind them, and all the other characters who have something about them.

'So, I thought, the structure would follow the themes, or the catchphrases, coming from these people. But I say: "let's not stop there: let's dive down into business stuff so the people that are interested in, you know, first line management, or even further up the tree of second or middle-line management, may say, there's some nice little anecdotes there, I can pick up a thing or two from them. It's obviously worked for Bill because he's ended up owning two companies but he started out as a man on the street, you know, just pouring oil over machinery."

'Then I'll move on to someone like, Roy Standon, who was incredibly inspirational for me and his little tagline was: "Well, you need to take a wider view on things," and he then referenced me to another guy we worked with and said: "You know, the problem with you, Dave, is, you're not like Bill. Bill takes a wider view on things," and I thought, what the hell's he talking about, I take a wider view?

'So, I said to him: "Why did you say that?" He said: "Because, you always ask questions and you get more information," and so the chapter where Roy's concerned, is all about how you're more powerful asking questions than you are answering them. 'So, what comes from all of this?

'You start looking at the academic-type stuff in that chapter, then you see how you could ask questions. You might opt for Porter's 5 Forces model and start to understand, you know, the dynamic market you're working in, or you could, if you're building a business plan, look at PEST – Political, Economic, Social, Technological – analysis, so, you could ask yourself questions under those headings. The more questions you ask, the more powerful you become.

'And then there's another great character, Bill Budden, a wonderful guy. We could talk about him for such a long time, but at the end of the day, his total philosophy is, you know, walk along the beach and think it through. Only this afternoon I've had some guys saying: "What are we going to do about this client?"

'I was able to say to them: "Listen, nothing's going to happen this afternoon, it's Friday, and we've got a Bank Holiday, let's sleep on it, let's think it through." There's many a time where people really want to be spontaneous and decisive and say: "Yeah, let's go and do that," and then, before you know where you are, you're all getting shot.

'So, as I say, there's valuable lessons all the way through this set of stories. There is a headline, or governing thought for each of them.

'When I was starting to write all these things down I started to think, there's so much here.

'Often, you know when people get a bit older, companies make them redundant and then the same managers turn 'round and say we've got no experience left in the company. In the end, of course, taking the wider view you might say, we all get made redundant. That is life.

'The experience goes to the grave and if you are sensible you might think to yourself, oh, that's an awful shame; as I was able to say only this afternoon to my younger colleague: "Look, Ollie, think about it, sleep on it, we've got until Tuesday, we don't have to jump through hoops right now because things, you know." He said: "Yeah, yeah. You're right, you're right." If everyone wants to leap in, the chances are there'll be a mess.

'Now then, what have we got this week in the UK? The big is-sue, up until a few weeks ago that everyone was talking about, was sustainability, carbon footprint, net zero. No doubt it's the big topic.

'Then, all of a sudden, no-one's talking about that! They're all talking about inflation, and so now everyone's saying: "Oh my God," you know, "How are we going to deal with this?" So I say to the guys: "Do you know what? Unfortunately, I've lived through that. I had a mortgage that was 15% and 17%, you guys haven't got a clue."

'You've got to keep adapting. Working in a high inflation envi-ronment is a lot, lot more difficult than one with no inflation. That's why everyone wants zero inflation because it makes commerce a helluva lot easier.

'With high inflation you've got to react more quickly. They're all running around now, of course, that companies' viability is at risk due to inflation. In our company for next year, we've got 60% of our workload already in the bag as forward orders. So, I've said to my directors: "That might look rosy to you, but remember, we might have got as much as 18% liability right there because of in-flation."

'They go: "What, Bill?" I say: "Well, yeah, exactly. And so, now, we've got to tighten the battens down, control costs like it's going out of fashion, look at the supply chain, you know, try and only focus on high margin stuff and also make sure that we're not quoting stuff with fixed prices that takes us through to 2025 – and all those sorts of things.

'And they're all: "Yeah, yeah, yeah, oh, we'd better have a meeting about it." I'm like: "We need to have an action plan, not a meeting!"

'There's so many things that I've done, that, whether or not peo-ple are interested I don't know, but I've done as a help for others like me, as well as for my own happiness; I want to do this.'

Contents

Silk Tie

CHAPTER ONE

Under dull January skies, Britain is bidding farewell to its wartime saviour, Sir Winston Churchill, at the world's biggest state funeral. A still youthful Edward Heath is taking over the reins of the Conservative Party, in opposition to the Labour government of Harold Wilson.

It is 1965. In May, The Rolling Stones release 'I Can't Get No Satisfaction', topping the charts in both the US and the UK.

Elsewhere, President Johnson is sending the first of what will be many thousands of US combat troops to Vietnam; Dr Martin Luther King is leading civil rights demonstrators from Selma to Montgomery, Alabama, and Lee Kuan Yew will withdraw from Malaysia to found an independent Singapore.

In the sporting arena, Muhammad Ali defends his WBC/WBA heavyweight boxing titles firstly against Sonny Liston, whom he knocks out, and secondly Floyd Patterson. While the Italians and the French fraternise in their newly bored Mont Blanc tunnel, the Post Office Tower opens in London – the capital's tallest building. It is a vintage year for films too with the release of *The Sound of Music*, starring Julie Andrews and Christopher Plummer, *Dr Zhivago*, starring Omar Sharif and Julie Christie, and *Thunderball*, starring Sean Connery as James Bond.

Meanwhile, a larky seventeen year old from Strand School (motto: 'Advance'), in the Tulse Hill area of South London, wonders just what he should do in life. There are strictly no flies on the young Bill Evans ('I had attitude: I was always asking questions'). He is a bright lad, has passed the 11+ to secure his Grammar School place and is studying for his O-levels. Then come the summer months and the waiting to get the results. As the summer progresses Bill spends a lot of time with his pals, learns to drive and tries to see acts like The Rolling Stones as often as he could.

'I'm sure there was a degree of (long-range) pressure from my father, who, by then, had gone to live in Wales on his own,' he recalls. '"Well, what job do you want to do – and so on?" I was particularly good in the sciences and even better in mathematics. So, I decided that I wanted to be a chartered accountant and that I think is what I grabbed at.'

Bill opted to go back to Strand School to continue his A levels in Pure Maths and Additional Maths. It was at this point that Bill's father stepped in with a powerful suggestion: 'I'd like you to go and meet my bank manager.' When Bill asked why, his father rejoined: 'Well, he's got a different opinion on maybe what you should be doing.' So, the young Bill did as he was bid.

'So, anyway off I trot to this, what I would classify not as an interview, but more of a chat with this bank manager, Mr Wilson, a very, very formal guy, at the bank in Roehampton. It is just a very small office with brown furniture, but this is the first time that I've ever had an interview.

'I don't even know what an interview is, so I am very nervous… So I go along and I have my school uniform on which is somewhat relevant to what I want to say later.

'I can see Mr Wilson right now; he has the black jacket on, the waistcoat with the gold fob watch, and the very traditional, sort of stripey, long, grey trousers… "spongebag" I think they call them… that the lawyers wear.

'The other thing is his bowler. Bowlers were definitely part of the uniform and so was an umbrella, by the way.

'But the thing that really takes my eye is that he has his handkerchief sticking out of his cuff, you know. I just think, why is it like that? It is all part of the uniform these guys have.'

From the off, Mr Wilson does most of the talking.

'He starts telling me,' recalls Bill, 'about the big benefit of going to work at Barclays Bank and one of the things was; he says if I join the bank I would then start doing my Institute of Banking examinations in lieu of doing my A levels.

'He says it would be more relevant for me. So, at the end of his talk, I just say: "Right, Okay."

As he leaves, Mr Wilson shakes Bill's hand firmly: 'Let me give you some advice, young man,' he declares solemnly. Bill asked: 'What's that, Sir?' Mr Wilson says: 'You know you're going to come and work in the bank and you need to be properly attired.'

Arriving back in Tulse Hill, the schoolboy is quizzed by his mum as to how the encounter has turned out.

Bill replies: 'Oh I think it went fine. I don't know if I'm getting a job but he told me that I need to be properly attired.'

His mum replies: 'Well, that's pretty obvious.' Bill protested: 'But I don't know what he means – "attired".' His mother soon put him right: 'Well you've got to dress accordingly.' Bill said: 'Well I know one thing Mr Wilson said: "If you can't be properly attired, the very least you can do is invest in a silk tie".'

When he tells her that he has to have a suit and tie his parents both start to laugh.

'There I am, 17 years of age,' recalls Bill, 'I haven't got a bloody clue what attire means or even what a silk tie is because I've never had one, I only have a school tie.'

It is at this point that his mum, a no-nonsense, practical woman, from whom Bill says he derives all his ability in Maths, takes matters in hand:

'Right,' she says, 'I'm going to take you up to London (South London is deemed to be way out of town) and get you your first business clothes so that you're properly attired.'

First, they go to Burtons in Streatham where Bill gets himself a tailor-made suit in dark blue. Not content with that, Bill's mother whisks him up to the even more upmarket Jaeger in Regent Street. 'In those days,' Bill explains, 'the banks were open on a Saturday, but you wore more informal clothes and I found out that you needed to wear a sports jacket on that day and a suit during the week.' Freshly attired, the young Bill Evans soon finds himself reporting for work in Barclays Bank, Northcote Road, Clapham Junction – with the very same Mr Wilson firmly in charge as its manager.

Mr Wilson has cultivated the habit of breezing into the branch

My mum, Helen May Evans, born on 9th May 1912 and married to my dad, Louis. Often called Ada by my friends, Mum looked after me until I was 20, when she left London to live with my dad in Wales. A very clever woman, she was ranked 6th out of all the school kids in Portsmouth where she grew up. She met my dad while he was in the Royal Navy. She also gave birth to two daughters who are much older than me. Mum went on to become a great grandma and an inspiration to Sue.

well after the doors had opened. The word goes around quietly: 'Mr Wilson's arrived.' He has an unmistakable – if not unshakeable – air of authority. Bill remembers that he calls everybody, without exception, Mr, Mrs or Miss.

A few days after he starts, Bill presents himself at the branch in what he thinks is a fine, button-down blue shirt. Almost immediately a low voice from the corner summons him: 'Mr Evans, come into my office'.

Young Evans: 'Yes Sir?' Mr Wilson: 'I'd like you to go home and change your shirt, you only wear a white shirt in my branch. Please go home now.'

Dumbfounded, the young Bill exits the boss's office only to blurt out to one of the ladies nearby:

'He's just sent me home!' The typist does not bat an eyelid: 'Oh yeah, well, we thought you'd be sent home. You were wearing a blue shirt. You don't wear blue shirts in Barclays Bank with Mr Wilson.'

So, off young Bill goes, all the way back home to Tulse Hill. Everything is happening to him all at once; learning how to drive, starting a new job, being told he can't wear a blue shirt, starting his career and also going to night school to study for the banking examinations.

He feels acutely embarrassed – as only a teenager can – and also, distinctly fearful because he thinks, 'Shit, am I going to lose my job then?'

Not owning a car means he first has to clamber onto the bus down to Clapham Junction, then take a train back to Tulse Hill, run up to his house and grab a new shirt. Four hours later, back he slinks back into the office, correctly attired in a pure white shirt.

From Mr Wilson there comes not the slightest reaction but everyone else in the office can barely contain themselves.

'The experience is still vivid,' recalls Bill. 'What I learnt from it was that your appearance is important. I didn't appreciate exactly what was being said at the time.

'It is summed up in an important maxim: "You don't get a second chance to make a first impression."

'That is the message that I was being given,' he says. 'You are a product. You're a product at Barclays Bank, you have to display the image of the bank as utterly professional and trustworthy. Your appearance sends out the message, it sends out a message of confidence. So, that is what they were trying to convey but didn't say to me in so many words.'

Bill admits to enjoying the early experience of military discipline at Strand School. While there, he joins the CCF, the Combined Cadet Force. On Fridays, cadets are allowed to wear army uniforms and after gaining certain proficiencies, cadets can upgrade to the RAF branch of the force.

In due course Bill becomes an RAF cadet – but one of the aspects of wearing uniform on Fridays is that it has to be immaculate. The boys have a dress assembly where the Major, when it is the turn of the army, and a Flight Lieutenant, when it is the turn of the RAF, inspect them to make sure that trousers are pressed, shoes are shiny, shirts are clean, ties knotted correctly and so forth.

'I've been drilled in this quite strict discipline, and I have to say, I used to love it,' recalls Bill. 'On a Thursday night, I got taught the trick of getting a real sharp crease in the trousers by putting soap inside the crease and then pressing it, so the soap actually makes it almost like a glue for your trousers.

'It was fascinating to spit and polish up the toe caps to perfection. We all wanted to have the shiniest mirror toes.

'All this stuff is being installed in me like software, and then I go to the bank and this guy's more or less saying to me this is our uniform.

'So I don't react when I am pulled up. Some kids might have said: "I'm not doing that", "Who's he telling me what to wear?", but I sort of buy into it. And the later thought of "You don't get a second chance to make a first impression" merges in my memory of what is actually going on in the workplace.

'The other thing I start to take out of all of this is that, as a banker, in the week you wear a suit and a silk tie and at the weekend, on a Saturday morning, you wear a sports jacket and maybe a tweed tie

RAF – Here I am dressed in RAF uniform. Strand School had a voluntary Combined Cadet Force (CCF). On Fridays we wore our military uniforms and got a chance to show off our mega shiny boots and razor-sharp trouser creases. That was the start of my being conscious of the need to dress smartly.

or something like that.

'So, the learning point for me is around adaptability to your environment.

'Later on, when I become a salesman, I start to realise that if I am doing business in the West End of London people will be dressed more casually, but if I go up to the City, it has to be a pinstripe suit. Nothing else will do. Bear in mind there are still plenty of bowler hats walking over London Bridge in the morning in those days.'

Bill starts to realise that he has to dress according to the circumstance because otherwise he could stick out like a sore thumb.

Being relentlessly inquisitive, he also buys John T Molloy's 1975 bestseller *Dress for Success* about the effect of clothing on a person's success.

He's already seen the famous Xerox salespeople at work: 'The guys that sold the photocopiers and stuff like that many years ago, had an edict from their head office that they all had to wear a navy blue suit, white shirt and a red tie. That was their uniform.'

For Bill, clothing is becoming part of a sophisticated toolkit. 'I realised,' he says, 'that we have a true opportunity with the way we dress to come over in different ways; for instance, do you want to be in a power situation or in a non-intimidatory one?

'Nowadays, if you want to go into a high-level meeting in the City, you might opt to wear a dark suit and a white shirt because that symbolises power. If, on the other hand, you go into an architect's office and you're wearing an open shirt and casual jacket, they will see you as being willing to collaborate.

'The way you dress really is important if you want to be a leader. It doesn't matter what level you are, but you simply have to think about that.'

When Bill Evans starts to lead his own large salesforce, the dress code becomes a central plank of his strategy. He invites a consultant from high street retailer Austin Reed to address one of the team meetings. In an early example of personal branding, the consultant gives a presentation on the values of what the company and sales team should present, what it should wear and when.

'We all know,' the Austin Reed consultant says, 'that you put your best suit on when you go to a wedding. 'But,' he says, 'you don't get a second chance to make a first impression. So, think about who you are going to go and see today, where am I going to go and see these people, do I wear a suit, or do I just come along in my tennis equipment?'

Environment has always been key. In the 1960s and 1970s one convention was: 'You never wear brown in town.' Bill recollects: 'I really thought that was funny when I first heard it. Then I thought to myself, do you know, you're absolutely right. You don't wear brown in town!'

More recently, however, Bill is the first to accept that dress codes and fashions have changed.

'We know fashion is cyclical,' he says, 'and we also know that fashion has been disrupted, if you like, by Covid and Working From Home. The fashion houses have developed lines of fashion now that are deemed to be semi-formal.

'Less formal clothing has also become more affordable and so it's quite possible that very formal wear – a full suit environment – may never exist again, that could well be the case. The world is a lot different in terms of communications, social media, and so on.

'The other important thing now is sustainability, and so recycling of clothing; do we throw away clothes prematurely?'

While much is changing, Bill says that should not detract from the message about what we should wear. He is adamant on the basic point that, at any given time or place, you remain the product.

'You have to treat yourself, manage yourself, as a product. You must think about how you would package the product. That insight all comes from Mr Wilson and the silk tie. That's how it all started.

'Throughout my career I've gone on to share the story of Mr Wilson a lot. But, unbelievably, just the other day one of my guys is on the video call and he's wearing a T-shirt. I actually just say to him: "Are you going off to play football?"

'I can see him on the screen and he looks back at me. I say: "You've got a football shirt on, mate!" I say to him: "You can't

Mr Wilson was the epitome of the 1950s/60s bank manager. In those days managers wore a distinctive uniform and carried accessories to carry off the look. The uniform comprised an umbrella, bowler hat, FT under the arm and fresh buttonhole, together with a waistcoat and pocket watch. Requiring high standards and formal in every aspect, I often ask myself, were they so wrong?

do that because you've got a customer meeting and even if you're on a screen you still have got to have a business shirt on".

'You can have no trousers, no-one's going to know that! But the top half of you has got to look right so even if you're working from home on a video, you've still got to look the part because you can't reverse what you've just done, you don't have that second chance.

'Oh my God, some of the guys I see on Zoom calls are so scruffy! Everybody knows I'm not asking people to go out and buy Savile Row suits or anything like that, but the message from Mr Wilson is, at the very least, get yourself a silk tie!

'White shirts don't cost much, simple shirts do not cost a lot of money. You've got to always be clean, tidy, and most importantly, in a face-to-face situation, your shoes have got to be clean.

'How many people go into somebody's office with mud all over their shoes? You just think to yourself, you wouldn't go into somebody's home like that so why would you turn up to some-body's office with mud on your boots? It doesn't give clients much confidence about the way you might look after a lift, does it?'

Bill goes back to Mr Wilson: 'He walked the talk. Looking back on it now, it was the era of stiff collars, so after this incident I even went and got one of these shirts where you had to put the brass stud in at the back and the front and you had all these different colours that you could put on.'

Bringing the silk tie story full circle, Bill says:

'At D2E we believe in dressing for our own success. We have our own work uniform. Everybody is issued with D2E branded work-wear and can request more items.

'Everyone has polo shirts with our logo, everybody has a fleece that works both out on site or in the office. Our team also have their own outerwear storm coats, and I always suggest to people, when you're on a Zoom working from home, put your polo shirt on, which I have to say 75% of them do naturally.

'So, while I'm an advocate of not making people feel as though they have to wear a uniform, I'd like to make them feel proud to show off the company.

'One more thing I'd like to cover is the wearing of ties. Yes, it is generally accepted in current working environments that we should all be tie-less. But I have to tell you that's not 100% correct for all clients. If you are dealing with international clients, especially those from Asia, they may still wear them.

'We had a situation only this year where we were invited to a meeting and the project manager who invited us to a meeting told us the clients were from Singapore. "Just a heads up," he said, "they will be insulted if you turn up without a tie." We said: "Really?" He said: "Oh yeah, they're very fastidious about things like that, they see it as a formal recognition."

'So it's back to my point: you have to look at the audience, who they really are, where they are from and how they dress. So the blanket "Oh we don't wear ties anymore" may not be what your clients expect of you. They're buying you as a product – so what do they expect? This is why you have to think about it rather than be blinkered about it.

'The whole point of all of this book is to explore the charisma of leaders, and the charisma of leaders is that they walk through the door and you say: "Oh I want to go and talk to that person."

'That's really what I'm trying to get over; you are a product and so therefore you need to create this magnetism.

'Now the magnetism doesn't work because you're a male model from Savile Row, but you send out this signal of power and that's what these remarkable people have all got in common. They walk through the door and you think, he's the boss.

'Mr Wilson would walk through the door and we'd all look at him and he'd say: "Good Morning", "Good Morning Mr Wilson, Good Morning, Sir" and all that. That's really what I'm trying to get over; how it all links together.

'So think about what you're doing, from the time that you start getting ready for work in the morning. Realise that you are a product and you've put thought into all of that.

'If you do, you will reap the benefits.'

Your appearance is a part of the message
you convey, it represents the product or the
company you work for, or how you want to be
known as a person. Use it strategically.

• • •

You don't get a second chance to make a first
impression.

• • •

Adapt your outfit/appearance to your clients,
your message, the dynamic you want to create
(power vs. not intimidating), the timing
(weekend vs. week) and your environment.

• • •

Make sure your team proudly represents
your company.

• • •

The same rules also apply for online meetings.

Morning, Alright?

CHAPTER TWO

The sixteen Art Deco residential blocks of Dolphin Square hulking over the streets of Pimlico have a storied past.

Completed in 1937 by John Costain, over what had been Thomas Cubitt's sprawling workshops a decade earlier, the newspapers of the time call it 'the most distinguished rental address in London'. During the Second World War the Square becomes by turns an ambulance station, hospital and headquarters of General de Gaulle's Free French.

Surviving no fewer than three bomb hits as well as numerous post-war changes of ownership, the Square's sound-proofed, self-contained flats are home to royalty, MPs, writers, actors and at least one spy from the Profumo era.

Yet in 1967, the year of the Six Day war, there is another game of cat and mouse waiting to be played here.

A fresh-faced Bill Evans, just twenty, is getting to the end of his tether.

His meagre salary at Barclays Bank – paid by age, not ability – is going nowhere fast. He's not even due for the next raise till he's 28. So, impatient to boost his earnings, young Bill applies for a job at American Express as a trainee money dealer in the City of London.

It is, he says, a big mistake.

'I just didn't know what I was walking into,' he admits. 'Commercial banking is a completely different world and it isn't long before I realise that I really don't like it. There is no people interaction. As a trainee you are at the beck and call of the dealers – and you have to work excessively long hours just to keep up with them.

'It's getting towards the end of my probationary period when I can still give one week's notice. After that I have to give a full month's notice and it became an obsession with me that I have to get out.

'So, I start applying for jobs all over the place and in those days applying for jobs is sending out letters and waiting for answers – it isn't quick.

'I go for one interview as a salesman for typewriters and the guy more-or-less laughs in my face when I turn up. He takes one look and says: "I really don't think you're old enough to be a salesman yet."'

Crestfallen, Bill signs on for the dole. In 1967 this means lining up at the local Labour Exchange in Brixton. It is one of the lowest points in Bill's life to date. 'I just feel really, really bad and I just think, you know what, this is never, ever going to happen to me again, I will never, ever be out of work.'

Later he meets up with his friend Roy who is working with the elevator company, Otis. 'Why don't you come and see what we're doing if you've got nothing to do?' says Roy, his face all smiles.

Shortly afterwards, Bill goes to Millbank by the Houses of Parliament to watch Roy and a colleague install a lift.

'Roy turns round to me and says: "Why don't you join Otis? They take anybody." So I say: "Really?" He says: "Yeah, they take anybody."'

The following day, Bill is impatient to phone the number he's been given.

'I get through to this guy... about 9 o'clock in the morning... and I say: "I've been given your number to see if you've got any jobs as fitters' mates".' Bill has already worked out he is too old at 20 to qualify for an apprenticeship but, paradoxically too young to qualify as a fitter's mate, so he has to add a year to his age on the application form.

'So there I am, phoning the guy up, and he says: "Yeah, we're looking for people at the moment – can you come for an interview?" I say: "Yeah, which day?" He says: "Well come today, come at 11 o'clock." I say: "Oh, okay".'

Back in Tulse Hill, Bill rapidly works out where the Otis Elephant and Castle office is. Pulling on his suit, he races down the road, onto the bus, arriving at the Elephant and Castle barely 30 minutes later and bursts into the Otis offices. 'I've come to see Mr Lindsey,' he pants.

'"Oh," they say, "he's gone out." I say: "Well he just told me to come for an interview." "Oh yeah, are you the guy with all the qualifications?" So I say: "Maybe." So they say: "Oh yeah, you need to see this guy, Dick Gaywood."'

Bill duly tracks down Mr Gaywood who promptly asks him: 'Now, who do you know?'

The young Bill replies: 'Well I know Alan Seaton, I know his dad, Ernie Seaton, I know his uncles, Tom Seaton and Burt Seaton, I know Roy Pluck and another guy, Micky Hill.'

'Oh,' says Mr Gaywood. 'Well, okay, you've got a start on Friday, 8 o'clock.'

Unable to believe his ears, Bill thinks the contrast with the banking world could not be more stark: this is boom-boom-boom.

Arriving punctually on the Friday morning, Bill is told to go to the stores where, 'a guy will pick you up'. 'They don't give me a name,' he recalls.

'There I am, standing there at 8 o'clock in the morning, really petrified of what is about to happen. In breezes this guy with a spare motorbike crash helmet in his hand and turns round to me. He says: "Are you Bill Evans, the bloke with all the qualifications?"

'So I say: "Yeah." He says: "Have you got all your qualifications with you?" So I say: "Well, no, I didn't know I had to bring them with me." He says: "Alright, put this on, you're coming with me." So, this is the start I have… learning to live in the construction world rather than the banking world.

'I get on the back of his motorbike, and Jimmy Giles drives me straight to Dolphin Square. That's where I work for the next three and a half years.

'Now Jimmy,' says Bill, '…At first I think he is a bit of a nutcase, though at the end of the day he looks after me. But, My God, does he give me a ride for those three and a half years!

'He is ex-army, always very smart. In those days we have a uniform that you more or less have to plead for – an Otis uniform. It's a green jacket and Jimmy prides himself in putting all the creases down the sleeves, very army-style.

'Jimmy isn't very technically orientated but nonetheless what I learn from him is absolutely invaluable in my future career. He is a proud family man, of Irish descent, and one of the things that I learn is to be resilient to the way that he used to have "downs".

'I would come in at 8 o'clock and he wouldn't be there. There would be a note for me: "gone up to Victoria Street to a site there, meet me up there".

'I'm thinking, shit, I've come late! And I'm looking at my watch, no, I haven't come late, so here we go, up I go to Victoria Street, get into the lift motor room and there'd be another note, "gone to Lloyds Bank".

'He would play me like that many a time. It would go on like that for two days on end. It was his funny game – God knows what turned him on – but he would just literally leave me trails to follow to wherever he was.

'Then, all of a sudden, he'd leave another note: "I'm working in Dolphin Square, Hood House, in the motor room" and I'd go down there and there he would be.

'He'd say: "How are you?" So I would say: "I've been looking for you for a couple of days." He'd shoot back: "Well, you weren't quick enough were you?"

'So, I would just think, "Holy Shit!"'

If Bill is feeling unsettled, his parents are horrified that he is out of work and then even more appalled that he has not merely left the banking world and Institute of Banking Examinations, but is ending up a humble fitter's mate.

By this time, both parents have gone to live in Wales, leaving Bill to fend for himself in Tulse Hill. On a rare visit back to South London his mother asks: 'Well what sort of money are you going to be earning?'

Bill replies: 'Well I don't really know, but I do know it's much better than working at American Express.' In those days, Otis employees are paid cash by registered envelope, after deductions

Alan Seaton, an old school friend from The Strand, came from another family of Otis inevitables. Alan started his apprenticeship there, where else? After my stint at The Banks, Alan and Roy Pluck convinced me to join Otis. 'They take anybody,' he said. We have been lifelong friends ever since. When D2E began Alan retired from Otis to join me. Thanks, Alan.

for tax.

'Since my mother happens to be there the week I get paid, I say to her: "Well, open it up", because I know how much it's going to be. She opens it up and it's £33.00 and she says: "I can't believe you're doing this job for just £33.00."

'So I say: "Mum, that's one week's money." There I was working at American Express previously and I got £60.00 clear for the month and here I am at Otis, in my first week, clearing £33.00.

'She says: "That can't be right, you can't be earning that sort of money doing that sort of job." I say: "Yeah I am." She says: "Well that's unbelievable." So I say: "Well, I know, but we have to do the work and..." Anyway, so she is finally okay.'

So what does Jimmy Giles really teach the young Bill Evans? 'The most important thing of all,' says Bill, 'is that in all that time, I don't think we are doing much work. I'm just thinking, when are we going to do some work?

'His style is all about the customer because every single morning, apart from when he's playing games, we walk around Dolphin Square.'

'At the time the Square is one of the largest apartment blocks in the whole of Europe, with 29 lifts split into 13 different houses. Each house has two lifts and there is also a hotel section.

'We walk around and we go and see the porters of each of the houses every morning and Jimmy says: "Morning, Alright?"

'They say: "Morning Jimmy, Morning Bill, everything's fine." He'd say: "Okay, well if you've got any problems you let me know tomorrow, won't you?" "Yeah, yeah, yeah." Well, we walk around the whole estate and that's all we do, every day, and he would be talking to the customer every day. His initiative is to avoid any complaints being reported back to the Otis office.

'He has it completely under control. If there is anything wrong, they write it on a bit of paper and say: "Oh Jimmy the indicator lights aren't working on the 7th floor."

'He has 14 porters more-or-less working for him! It is just amazing to watch, we never have any breakdown calls phoned through to the office, never! We always have an issue flagged directly from the end user. But I think to myself at the same time, is this work?

'Of course, subsequently, I realise that if you put your face in front of the customer then you're going to avoid any issues, you're going to pick up opportunities, and when I look back on it you can't ask for anyone to be more customer-orientated than Jimmy.

'Jimmy is walking around and seeing the porters. He's got eye contact with them and he's seeing the people that are really important. He's right at the sharp end of the information because, as you know, as things get cascaded up or cascaded down, they get filtered.' As Bill begins to take on responsibility for customer satisfaction later in his own career, he has reason to be thankful for the early lessons he has learnt in Dolphin Square.

In 1993, when Bill has already turned 45, he finds himself in another London square, this time Paternoster right by St Paul's Cathedral. A vital Otis customer is becoming exasperated and it happens to be the leading UK general contractor, Bovis.

Bill takes up the story: 'They are really, really upset with Otis' performance. You know, somehow, my intuition is to get up early, go there and just sit outside the construction site hut to see the big boss.

'So, this particular morning I get up to Paternoster at 7.30 in the morning and, with the "Morning, Alright?" philosophy in my head, I'm sitting there and the security guard says to me: "Who've you come to see?"

'So I say: "I've come to see Peter Fisher." The guard says: "Oh, he's one of the directors at Bovis." So I say: "Yeah, I want to see him."

'Anyway, so this Peter Fisher turns up and he says, "Who are you?" So I say: "I'm from Otis." He says: "Oh yeah? We're not really happy with you."

'I say: "I know, that's why I've come. I want to hear what we've got to do." So, Peter Fisher lists out all the stuff that needs fixing and I go away and put an action plan in place and – within two or three weeks – we fix it all.

Jimmy Giles of Otis: what a character! Past master of the wind-up, he came from an Otis family: dad Gilo, the ropey, and brother Billy, a repairman. Jimmy loved working at the exclusive Dolphin Square, whose colourful patrons suited him down to the ground. Among the other things we got up to was setting up a secret dump where we brewed our own beer. There's a lot else I could relate but daren't. Suffice it to say it was all part of growing up for me.

'About a month later I get a phone call from Les Chatfield, the managing director of Bovis and he says: "You're Bill Evans?" "Yeah, I'm Bill Evans." He says: "Are you the guy that went to see Peter Fisher up at Paternoster?" So I say: "Yeah, I'm hoping that everything's been resolved."

'He says: "Yeah, it's all been resolved, but I just want to phone you up." He says: "You're the first person from Otis at senior level that's ever bothered to come and see us and you fixed the problem and I just want to thank you for that." So I say: "Well obviously, it's my job."

'So he says: "Right I want to meet you and I want to meet you with another client, Stanhope, and I want to talk about a lot of work we've got on and it's really important that we get engaged with you and Stanhope."

'So I meet up with the boss of Stanhope, who happens to be a guy called Peter Rogers, brother of Richard Rogers, the architect, who's sadly just passed away.

'Needless to say, I'm now in giddy-height-land.

'Anyway, fast-forward with all the discussions and, as a result of that early morning call to Paternoster Square, we, at Otis, are able to sign a partnership deal with Stanhope Bovis for £25 million's worth of business. £25 million's worth in one year!

'It all starts by getting up in the morning early and going to see the customer, right? Many people will say, well, of course customers are important. But you know you're only judged by your actions, not by your words.'

Later on Bill is sent to the IMD in Switzerland for a management training programme. One of the sessions at the business school is on customer satisfaction.

'It is absolutely fascinating for me,' Bill remembers. 'Here I am thinking, do you know what? I am customer orientated!

'It's nice to get the right feedback to endorse what you feel but you don't want to end up truly believing your own propaganda. Nevertheless, I have to say that when I started listening to all the stuff about customer satisfaction it is something that I truly believed in.

'The lecturer is talking about many different examples of customer satisfaction and he references Tom Farmer, the guy that started up Kwik Fit, the tyre company.

'He is talking about how that company thrives on customer satisfaction and how it is their only metric. So, when I get back from Switzerland I think, you know, I am going to go and see this guy.

'Anyway, I phone up Kwik Fit in Edinburgh and I say I'd like to speak to Tom Farmer and they say: "What's that about?" I say it's about customer satisfaction and I've heard from the IMD that he's been referenced in this book called "Total Customer Satisfaction" and I'd really like to exchange ideas with him.'

Bill soon finds himself invited up to meet with Tom Farmer himself in Corstophine in Edinburgh.

Bill recalls: 'Tom is happy to talk through Kwik Fit's philosophy and how, when they change a set of tyres, then as far as he's concerned it's not satisfying the customer because if you're really satisfying the customer you're always going to be doing something more than what they expect.

'So,' Tom Farmer says: 'Come with me.'

They both go down to the local depot of Kwik Fit and walk around while Farmer shows Bill Evans multiple examples of how Kwik Fit manages the business. The most important thing to Farmer is providing customers with more than they expect.

'He says, if customers are happy with the "more" that you give them, then they're satisfied and they're going to give you a reference.

'The first innovation he puts in is a waiting booth and the second thing he does is offer free coffee, but the third thing is that there is a phone call 24 hours later saying: "We hope you were satisfied with our service."

'So, they kick in the whole process and if there is any commentary about dissatisfaction that is registered, and then every month, Tom Farmer would get a rating of all his depots around the UK on which depot is dipping in customer satisfaction.

'The depot manager has to put the whole of his staff through customer training in their own time in order to get the score up and if you don't get the score up after three months the depot manager would be replaced.

'So, there is a degree of autocracy there, like, you will improve customer satisfaction for sure. That is how they would do it.'

When Bill starts his own business, D2E, the single most important thing to him and the one metric that the company really cares about is customer satisfaction.

Three years after the launch, D2E instigates Zoomerang surveys (now called Survey Monkey).

'At D2E,' Bill contends, 'we send an annual customer satisfaction survey to all our clients. Religiously, for every one of the last fifteen years, we've been monitoring our customer satisfaction rating, using, for consistency, exactly the same questions every year.

'That's why we're able to plot the improvement or degradation of all the different subjects that we survey.

'The feedback from the survey and the analysis is what we actually kick-off the meeting we hold every year in January with, at the beginning of our financial cycle. We actually present what the clients are saying and the areas that we need to improve.'

After gauging customer satisfaction, D2E also dissects the material from an objective mathematical standpoint while tempering the results examining qualitative responses, which Bill regards as the 'live commentary' on the business.

'We take those responses and we say, it's all very well them saying we're doing a good job, but we need to a better job!'

D2E also looks at the loss reports where Bill's team look for what he calls 'golden nuggets'.

'Alright,' he says. 'Emotionally you feel upset about the fact you lost a job but you also have to realise that market forces will always be just that. You'll never have 100% market share.

'But the most important thing is to learn from why you lost a job. 'I flatly refuse to accept we lose any job on price (more on that later) but the most important thing is using the customer input to grow your business, and whether it be bad news or good news, you want the qualitative information rather than just the simple "you lost it on price" or "you lost it because you were late" or "yeah you're doing a great job."

'At D2E we have put in action plans for retraining on project management, we've put in training for answering the phone, we've put in training for improving the way that we do our quotations, with the way we do reports – but without this customer satisfaction feedback, we wouldn't be continuously improving our offer.

'As a consequence, the company is growing and we only use customer satisfaction as our metric. We don't have financial objectives because they fall out of the customer satisfaction.'

'So, thanks to Jimmy back in the day, getting up early, going round, seeing the porters, "Morning, alright?" and then taking that in to getting up early and going to see Bovis, and then realising that customer satisfaction is the key to a successful business, this is where D2E has flourished – as a direct consequence of their input.'

ON CAR PARKS AND CUSTOMERS

"The learning at the IMD about customer satisfaction was fantastic,' recalls Bill. 'One story in that learning was around the signs and symbols of customer orientation.

'The lecturer, Jacques Horovitz, gave this story about when he was invited to go and do some work. He's the consultant brought in by Disney to resolve the issue of Euro Disney because it was a disaster when they first opened up.

'This guy went in, looked at the issues and so on. He became quite a famous customer satisfaction management consultant.

'One of the stories, which I love, is that he gets a call one day from this organisation over in Switzerland, flies over, gets into Geneva, picks up a hire car and he arrives at this big firm in Switzerland to meet up with the CEO.

'So, in he goes in to meet the CEO, good morning, coffee, dah–dah–dah, they have a little chat and Horovitz finally turns round to the CEO and says: "Listen I'm awfully sorry, I don't think I can work with you."

'So the guy says: "Why's that?" He says: "Because you've asked me to come out and help you with customer satisfaction, but I don't really believe that you're going to be open for my suggestions." So the CEO says: "Why's that?"

'He says: "Well, look. Look outside the window." So the CEO looks outside the window and Horovitz says: "What do you see?" So he says: "I see the carpark, I see the weather." So Horovitz says: "What's the weather like?" He says: "It's pouring with rain." So Horovitz says: "Yeah, and that's why I don't want to work with you." So, the boss says: "What do you mean?"

'He says: "Where have I had to park my car?" The

CEO says: "In the customer parking over the other side of the car park." So Horovitz says: "Yeah, and where's your Porsche?" The CEO said: "It's outside the door." So Horovitz says: "Well, if you switch the car parking arrangement around I'll come back and I'll work with you."

'So the guy says: "Are you serious?" So he says: "Yeah I am. If you're customer orientated you put your customer parking at the front by the door so they don't get wet."

'So when I come back to the UK I meet the Otis UK CEO, Jack Leingang, and I tell Jack the story. I say: "Jack we push our customers into the road, into Handforth Road but all the Directors have got all their cars right outside Clapham Road. We need to sort that out."

'Jack says: "Fix it." I went to the office manager and I say: "By the way you need to put two white squares outside the front door and clearly put in there Customer Parking." Cecelia says to me: "Are you serious?" I say: "Absolutely, you can phone Jack up if you like, he's authorised it."

'We do it, we change it. That's how we send a message to everybody that we are open for trading with customers and they'd get entry to our office without getting wet. It's a sign and a symbol that you truly believe in customer satisfaction. You've got to do simple things, but the value is very high.

'You can see things, like you can go into offices and you can see this is our customer charter, right, and I look at it and I think what's the point of that? "We are customer orientated." It means nothing! You have to do something that is tangible, that you can relate to rather than having a big poster on the wall. "We believe in customers." Okay, well prove it. It's an action thing, not a verbal thing.'

Have a learning attitude. Find the lessons in "negative" situations and follow topics that spark your interest.

• • •

Treat clients (and people in general) with a lot of care and respect. Prioritize, be personal and humble, over-deliver and act rather than talk.

• • •

Be effective rather than busy.

• • •

Know that every situation and connection can be important (even if it doesn't seem like it in the moment) and treat them as such.

• • •

Stay close to and maintain the projects and relationships that you care about, even when everything is okay, so you can spot small flames right away and they don't turn into big fires.

Getting a Wider View

CHAPTER THREE

By the late 1970s, London, particularly its war-torn financial district, the City of London, is changing out of all recognition. Medieval street patterns and Victorian facades are giving way to the gleaming 600ft vertical lines and 47 storeys of the Natwest Tower (renamed Tower 42) designed by Colonel Richard Seifart and his partners, which remains for many years the capital's tallest building. Nearby, the brutalist baroque of the Barbican Estate by Chamberlin, Powell and Bon is completed over a Cripplegate ward that has been almost flattened by the Luftwaffe a generation before. London is opening up to all sorts of new cultural influences too:

the strains of punk rock bands like the Sex Pistols and The Clash break in on the melodies of glam rockers such as Queen, songsters such as Elton John, Eurovision pop group Abba, and reggae performers such as Bob Marley and Peter Tosh.

After chasing around after Jimmy Giles, Bill is still in South London, enjoying his own active social life and keeping busy as a fitter. Ambition, however, soon begins to weigh on his mind.

'I apply for a field manager's job, and in those days they are called supervisors,' he recollects. 'The manager interviewing me says to me that I am still too young and I don't have any experience, so my application is unsuccessful.'

Within six to eight weeks of being told that, Bill gets another call from Otis saying they have a new job for him to plug the missing experience. So, Bill is packed off to work in Portsmouth – minus, it must be said, a girlfriend of whom he is very fond. It is here that he works on the Canberra, the liner that would later become famous as a troopship in the Falklands Conflict. Upon his return Bill is immediately promoted to tester.

Surely enough, the opportunity of becoming a field manager comes around once again: this time Bill gets the job and for the next few years he is a supervisor. Then he hits a snag.

'When you are a field manager in those days,' Bill says, 'you're assigned to a salesman who looks after the same portfolio as the field manager. Unfortunately, the salesperson in my area, Ted Seymour, falls sick for a very long time.

'It is getting a little difficult because customers are starting to contact me and say: "What's going on here? We're not getting any response." In those days, don't forget, we have no emails. The customers say: "We're not getting any response to letters, we're not getting any response to phone calls either".'

More than a little frustrated, Bill approaches both the sales manager and the field manager in charge of London operations for help and asks:

'Look what are we going to do?' Both managers more-or-less shrug their shoulders: 'What can we do, Bill?'

Bill's response to that is forthright. 'I say: "I might as well do the fucking lot myself," and I walk away.'

Two days later there comes another phone call to Bill: 'Bill, about your offer...'

'And I say: "What offer's that?"

'They say: "Well you said that you might as well do the effing lot yourself."

'So I said: "Really?" Anyway, I come back in the office and they say: "Look we want to do an experiment: for the field manager to try and look after his own sales as well as field. It'll be for six months."

'So I say: "Yeah, I'd love to do that!"

'So there I am, married now to Sue, working in the City of London in EC3, EC4, a really prime area and I become, if you like, a pioneer for someone actually running their own small business unit in Otis.

'There is also the need to split the area in two, so they bring in a guy who they also think has high potential from Brighton to look after the other half of the area. I don't have the whole area to myself because I am doing the two activities.

'This guy Dave and I work together, covering the whole aspect, field operations as well as sales activity. Then it comes to the 6-month review.

'During the trial, Otis have restructured the operations in London, as three separate districts: the City, the West End and South London, each of which has its own general manager. So, by now we'd got a new manager: Roy Standen, who is actually appointed our general manager in the City. It is the right appointment too.

'Now Roy Standen is one of these people who, when they walk through the door, you actually feel their presence.

'Part of it comes from his early career in the navy. He is a regular man, around 5'10 in height, who is always immaculately turned out. He isn't trendy but he's very smart – in navy speak, "he looks sharp." He's still alive, and to this day if you meet him socially, he'll still be wearing the blazer and the grey trousers with the top pocket handkerchief. Even as an elderly gentleman he has kept that "uprightness."

'Back then, I wouldn't say he is ever overpowering. That's important, because when I meet him, he has an aura about him that is completely warm. Customers absolutely love him and there's another thing he does which is incredibly important – but might seem insignificant.

'Whenever he sees a client he takes notes, he always asks the client: "Is it okay if I take notes?" It's a signal back to the client: "I'm receiving you, I'm hearing you, I haven't just stopped talking, I'm actually listening to you."

'He always has these little post-it type things inside his pocket. Not the big yellow ones but the little notelets, and he gets them out, starts writing and then refers to them afterwards. He is a professional man, and as I say, no-one ever speaks unkindly about him.'

Back to London 1978, Roy Standen finally gives his verdict on the trial. The feedback to Otis senior management is that it's not working because Dave is unable to manage the two roles, whereas Bill can.

Management inquires why is Bill Evans is able to perform whereas

Sue and Bill Evans. At our first business dinner. Thanks to Roy Standon's good guidance, we definitely looked the part. Sue has kept the dress as a momento, and quite right too: it's a great dress.

his colleague cannot. Standen's response is: 'Simple, Bill Evans takes a wider view of everything, he sees the bigger picture. The other guy can't seem to get away from just a single focus.'

'So, there I was,' recalls Bill: 'Ordained into this role and they made me the permanent field and sales guy for the whole City area. 'That's what starts my career working with Roy Standen. He takes a liking to me because he says: "There's a lot of things you need to learn." So I say: "Okay." He's the first guy that introduces me to customer entertaining, so I have my first customer lunch organized by Roy.

'Working with him, it is a lot of fun along Fenchurch Street and Leadenhall Street and Leadenhall Market and being in the thick of EC4, as well as right the way over to the Temple.

'There is a mixed customer bag there but we have the tall buildings of Kleinwort Benson, the bank at the time, Commercial Union and the old Baltic Exchange; the building later blown up by the IRA. Then of course we have Trinity House which looks after lighthouses and clients like that. Centrepoint, I think, is built around that time too.

'While I am there, the old Lloyds building is demolished and the new Lloyds building is constructed to the famous design of Richard Rogers. So we have really top-class clients. This is how I first come across Land Securities. My association with them goes back to 1978 and here I am today at D2E in 2022 and Land Securities happens to be one of my most important clients, 40 years later!

'This is the period when I put in the groundwork for me to get recognition. I actually was the first person in the UK to sell Elevonic control systems in the Kleinwort Benson and Commercial Union buildings. As a result I was promoted and moved to the Brighton office to become a branch manager, which we will talk about later. 'So those are my Otis clients in the late 1970s, right the way down to Tower Bridge and in the estate around the Tower. I have another story about the "silent close."

'Roy is a great coach too. At one time we are discussing a significant maintenance contract that we are renegotiating, or, more to the point, that I am trying to renegotiate. I suppose I am a bit naïve, but in a positive sense, because the uplift on the maintenance contract is significant.

'So Roy says to me, he says: "I think I'd better come with you." So I say: "Okay, right." So there we are and I'm doing all the talking, the client is asking a few questions. It comes to the close, the sales close, and the client says to me: "You know, this is a considerable uplift in price."

'I don't say a word, I just sit there and look him in the eye, waiting for him to say something more, and Roy doesn't say anything, and there is this silence that seems to go on forever.

'Then the gentleman says: "Well, it looks as though I'm going to have to agree to it." I say: "Okay, you have to sign at the bottom there," and he signs at the bottom of the agreement and as we walk out Roy says to me: "How the hell did you not say anything?" He says: "That was absolutely amazing. I have never experienced a salesman using the silent close like that."

'Well, at the time, I do not know what he means, I've never heard of the "silent close" but of course I do now – and I know now you have to shut up, you just have to be quiet, stop talking. So, I begin to realise that there is a skill in being quiet and I've used that skill many a time since, just to let the other person do the talking.

'The other thing that Roy does for me is to get me close to customers. He says one day: "Do you play golf?" I say: "No I don't." He says: "Well, the company have got a golf event and you need to come along." I repeat: "Well, I don't play golf." He says: "Don't worry, I can put you on what we call 'the shortest hole competition' so you're measuring who gets to the hole in one or nearest to the hole in one." That way he forces me into the customer environment and he gives me more and more confidence in being with customers at different events and so on.

'Getting back to Roy's wider view, however, you've got to develop this awareness when you're in business with the bigger picture, you've got to get the wider view.

'With Roy I started to realise that getting the wider view was

Roy Standen. Loved by customers, work colleagues and his Naval compatriots alike. Roy received recognition for services to the Royal Navy Reserves with an invite to the Queen's garden party at Buckingham Palace, as well as receiving the Queen's Silver Jubilee medal. Among his lesser-known achievements is that he got me onto the golf course for the very first time.

all about asking questions – and there's an old maxim that says, the power's in the question, not in the answer.

'Only yesterday, I ask one of the people working for me: "Are you prepared for the meeting?" She says: "Yep, I've got the presentation." I say to her: "No. What are your big questions? What are your five big questions you're going to go with, because at the end of the day this meeting has to be 80/20: 20% you, 80% them." That's the way you will get the bigger picture.

'So I've worked on it a lot over the years, even in a social environment, when you're chatting, whether it be in the pub or a restaurant or around somebody's house…I just love putting onto the table a big question to say: "How are you planning your holiday?" Trying to see which questions you can use to divert the chat away from all the usual nonsense into something more interesting.

'I get a lot of pleasure in playfully steering conversations without people even realising it.

'As you get more and more involved in running a company, it becomes even more important to get the wider view. Fortunately for me I've been in management schools, in Switzerland, the US, and France and time and time again they bring up the tools to do this, the tools which have stood the test of time.

'One of them is the PEST analysis: looking at political, economic, social and technology trends. That's one you can apply to analyse your business environment. If we were to talk about today, we might say political scene is highly volatile, the economic situation is precarious, socially we're moving in a world dominated by social media, and technology's developing mega-mega fast. So how you adapt your business to that bigger, changing picture is critical.

'Then of course you've got Porter's Five Force Analysis which is all about the competitive environment – and all the threats to your business. That's another great tool to use.

'One threat might be new entrants: in other words, can somebody come in, without you even realising it? Can somebody over in California develop an app and, all of a sudden, take away your business? Take Uber. They're a new entrant to the taxi business, and they've destroyed the traditional black cab segment purely because they've got the app.

'Another example might be: could somebody come along with a substitute product? The one that springs to mind is, you've got a petrol car and somebody comes along with an electric car, so they've substituted the traditional product for a new product – and what has that done? It's killing off the oil industry for one thing so, they're having to look at that. You've always got to look whether there is going to be a different way to do what you're doing. Are you aware of what that might be?

'Then another issue is about the power of suppliers. You might be in the supply chain but if you look further down that chain, there may be a big issue. There is currently one with the delivery of motor vehicles. There's no problem with manufacturing in German factories, but their assembly lines are stifled because, at the time we are speaking, they can't get their wiring out of Ukraine. So, the power of the supplier can affect you, and another factor is how much power the buyer has.

'When you've got all these different threats and power balances, and you examine them – you start to grasp the nature of the competitive environment you're in. If you compare yourself to another competitor, are they too experiencing the same threats and power imbalances?

'Coming down a level, onto tactics – and back to my experience working with Roy Standen – is that often you'd go into a meeting with a client, and you've prepared your pitch or your presentation and then you've got it completely wrong. The reason you've got it completely wrong is because you didn't get the buyer's shopping list.

'The great story here is the salesman selling an umbrella. The person goes in to buy the umbrella and the salesman says: "It's got an incredibly wide span, it's really colourful, the handle is lightening-proof because, when you're on the golf course, you want to make sure that you're not going to get an electric shock through the umbrella, it's very durable and all the rest of it."

Greenwich Maritime Museum: this was the grand and memorable venue for Sue's and my first big business dinner. The occasion was a concert by the famous cellist, Rostroprovitch. While it was a heavy-duty introduction to symphonies it was here that I began to learn the art of networking. To be honest, we found Wimbledon and Roland Garros a lot more to our taste.

'The customer then says: Do you know what, that's absolutely great but I don't want the umbrella for the rain or the golf!" So the salesman says: "What do you want it for?" He says: "Well I'm going on holiday, I need to protect my baby from the sun."

'So, you know, you can get it completely wrong, you go straight into your pitch and you've got it wrong.

'That's where the wider view can help: have you asked the right questions, have you got the customer's shopping list? What are they concerned about? Are they concerned about the economic situation and so on?

'A further basic tool along these lines is the SWOT analysis, S W O T: strengths, weaknesses, opportunities and threats.

'The traditional tools we just listed are really useful, really powerful, especially when you're building a business plan. But the other thing about taking a wider view is that you must keep pace with what's going on in the world today.

'One of the things that I've picked up in my latter career journey is this thing called the Executive Book Summaries, and the Executive Book Summaries is a fantastic subscription to an organisation that gives you all the latest business books in summary form, three books a month, and it's eight pages.

'It gets to the relevance of what's going on and so I've been consistently using that sort of stuff to try and keep ahead. It doesn't matter how old you are – you have to keep fit. A footballer doesn't go and play a premiership game without training, similarly, you don't go on stage without doing rehearsals.

'You can't be in the "when I" club: "when I was a fitter," "when I was a supervisor," "when I was a field manager... this is how it was". Yes, you can use those experiences but you also have to adapt them to the modern world, you can't constantly refer back and expect it to be the same.

'So Roy was, and is, a great guy. He would talk about people always listing problems, he would say: "I don't want to listen to problems, I only want to listen to solutions." He would say: "Your job is to be a solution provider, not a problem identifier, that's your job." The other thing he'd say was: "Out of adversity there's an opportunity." This is so true: it comes from being aware of the bigger picture and seeing opportunities to take advantage of.

'Simple thing: we've just gone through the Covid and a lot of the hospitality sector have really suffered through the Covid, but the smart guys have adapted, they say: "Right we can do a take-away service, we can do easy-to-get-our-menus."

'So, all of a sudden, the QR code, which stands for "quick response", means they're adapting their menus. So you can flash on the QR code and get the menu, you can get one of these new people – whether it be Uber Eats or Just Eats or one of these delivery firms, Deliveroo – and they are thriving on the adversity. Others have seen it differently: "Oh there's a big problem. I can't do this, I can't do that."

'There's even a big opportunity, dare I say it, in the dog industry because people all started getting dogs because of the lockdown. So now, what happens is, if you have a dog, you need dog parlours, you need more vets.

'I'm a real big advocate of saying, okay well, what are the competition doing, we've got to always be better. Information is free and the most strategic advantage that any company will have today in this modern world is time. You've got to act fast because if you don't, the others will catch you up quickly. So you've got to realise when it's time to be expedient, you have to jump on it quickly but you can only do that if you've got all this information.

'The last time there was a recession we grew our business because we seized on the overhaul and refurbishment market. People won't be building. Now, here we are in 2023, a similar thing's starting to happen. There's different issues causing that dynamic but you have to say, we're not going to be doing so many new-build projects but we're going to be doing a lot of refurbs, and sustainability is driving that agenda really.'

"I've got to give you this throw-away story, it's all coming back to me now. So, we sell this new system, the Elevonic system, into Kleinwort Benson Bank and it's the first time that lifts started talking to the riders, you know, 'doors closing' 'going up' and all the rest of it.

The Chairman of Kleinwort Benson contacts the Chairman, Lord Samuel of Land Securities and says – I don't know if it's the exact quote: 'God, man can you please switch off that horrible voice, it's American'.

In those days the software is all American voiced, you know.

Zoom out, look at the bigger picture. It allows
you to spot opportunities and use them.

• • •

In a business setting, use tools like Porter's 5
Forces, SWOT and PEST analyses,

• • •

Stay up to date with today's world, even if you
have "experience".
Get clear on customers' needs. Information is
free, use it!

• • •

LISTEN. Show that you care and get clear on
others' (real) needs.
Take notes.

• • •

Get into customer entertaining
(get closer to them and their environment).

Let them do 80% of the talking.
Ask the right questions. –
'The power is in the question.'
Use silence, it is powerful.

• • •

Always put in the ground work; it might not
seem important now, but later it may be.

• • •

Speed is your biggest strategic advantage in
today's world. – Move fast.

• • •

Be a solution provider, not a problem
identifier. Perspective is everything.
Every setback is a new opportunity.

Walk Along the Beach

CHAPTER FOUR

On April 1st 1982, almost three years after Mrs Margaret Thatcher first sweeps to power, Argentine commandos land on the beaches of the Falkland Islands as part of Operation Rosario. Their action provokes the Falklands Conflict. War flares up in the Lebanon too with Israel invading the southern half of the country. In July Italy beats Germany 3-1 to take the FIFA World Cup in Spain. September sees Princess Grace of Monaco's funeral. Two months later Michael Jackson releases his sixth studio album, *Thriller*, which will go on to sell 110 million copies. By the end of the year China's population tops 1 billion.

By this time Bill Evans is 36, married to Sue and has a baby son. He is yet again reviewing his future.

After a highly successful stint in the City, working alongside Roy Standen, a fresh surge of ambition is starting to take hold.

'I am working for a guy who's been introduced into the layer between Roy Standen and myself as the sales manager and I'm thinking, I can't believe that I've got to work for him. As a person, he was okay but as a professional person he just wasn't inspiring.

'I'm very frustrated and I think, hello, what am I going to do about this? When you're at that age, you start to get itchy feet, so I start looking for another job and, oddly enough, I am offered two of them.

'One is the managing director of Fujitec Lifts. That obviously is a great leap forward but I have to stop and ask myself: "Is this the right thing today?" I have the wise counsel of a few people and they say: "You're crazy, it's a brand-new company with a totally Japanese attitude." Then I end up getting offered a job with Stannah Lifts as the branch manager up in Norfolk.

'At any rate, I think the word has got back to the "powers that be" to say we've got to do something for this guy – so I am offered a job as the branch manager down in Brighton.

'It's clear that they have created the position for me because they move the branch manager to the side to get me this job. So I go to work in Brighton. I go there... how can I say this?... having to stay in hotels and all the rest of it whilst I am making the transition – moving from our house down to Brighton. I'll be honest with you, this period of my career is probably the most exciting ever: it's just amazing.

'There's no interview, I am given the job. "We want you to go down there and your boss will be this guy called Bill Budden," they say. So the transition involves going to look for a house and all of those disruptive things. I've got a young baby and a relatively young wife, and off I go. So I'm now a manager which I am highly motivated by.

'My first meeting with Bill Budden is just something incredible because, as we've been saying through the whole book, you know when somebody walks through the door, you think "Wow!"

'This guy, Bill Budden, he has presence. There's so much about him. Again, he is very smart in his appearance, he has brilliant blue eyes and masses of grey hair. You look at him and you think, do you know what, that's the sort of guy I want to be, I want to be like him. So, the next journey starts.

'So there I am, taking over the reins of the branch in Brighton and there is so much contrast to what I am used to because, in London, you're a part of this massive machine and your job is to oil the cogs.

'Down in Brighton you are the machine, and you are the man. My initial way of operating down there is to stick my nose into everything, and probably I come across as bloody Action Man: I've come down here to sort them out, I've come down here to show that I'm the man from London and I can do this and I can do that.

'Obviously I am soon ruffling feathers because they are used to managing what was a deck chair business really.

'Anyway, so Bill Budden's the general manager for the whole of the southern area of Otis which stretches literally from Land's End right the way through to Dover, and then right the way up to

Bill Budden. Otis Portsmouth. I really enjoyed working for, and with, Bill. In my opinion he was years ahead of his time. Here we are at the launch of the first Otis service product. The inspiration behind this came from Barry Harden. We were down in Jersey, having overspent the budget and got locked in due to the fog. It really was a fabulous occasion.

Robin Cheeseright or should I say, Robbing Cheeseright, as we affectionately knew him, was sadly lost to us too early. Robin was a gentleman, a great listener, and a great thought provoker. He loved football, even supported Charlton – his one and only serious mistake! Family man, inspirational and charming. We all miss him.

Suffolk and Norfolk. He has a massive area. He doesn't have London but he's got everything else.

'So there are a lot of branches, and the way he operates is that he will visit the branch, or, more to the point, the branch manager, so that he'll glide into the office, sit down and say, in a very Hampshire accent by the way: "How's it going, my boy?"

'You just sit there and you start to talk and he'll just let you ramble on. He is very clever in the way that he'll just say: "And how is this person, and how is that person, and that person?"

'When I reflect on it, he never asks anything about work, he only asks about people. That starts to change, if you like, my approach because now, don't forget, I'm the manager, and so I suppose I've got to change from being this super sales guy in front of all the customers.

'He's saying: "Don't forget: your job is to manage people, not manage the task." Of course, I am still very task management orientated because that's where I come from. Here he is telling me I'm not really interested in the task, I'm only interested in how you're managing the people.

'So this is the first time that I get introduced to "management by objectives" and it is something that I don't understand at first but obviously it starts to make sense after a period of time; that you set somebody a task which is very much a day-to-day thing, whereas an objective is much broader and long-term.

'So, Bill introduces me to management by objectives. The other profound thing he says is: "You need to think about what you're doing, you're too reactive, you're too on top of everything."

'He says: "Listen, take my advice, go for a walk along the beach and just think things through!" It is quite interesting because I am so action-orientated, I actually think he literally means just that: "Walk along the beach."

'But what he is trying to say to me is when you're thinking, you're actually working. Whereas, in my world, coming from London, you're only working when you've got something in your hands or you're doing something. I couldn't relate to "walk along the beach." 'Years later, when I start working with Robin Cheese-right, Robin uses a phrase, "let's sleep on it" and "you don't have to make a decision immediately" because the whole thing is you have to evaluate it all. But what Bill is trying to channel my thinking towards is: "You're managing people and you need to think about how you're managing people – and each person is an individual." So the way that you manage one person is not necessarily the way that you manage another person.

'If you look at a bunch of athletes you can have sprinters and the marathon runners at opposite ends of the spectrum. The objective for the sprinter and the marathon runner – the ultimate objective of both athletes – is to win the race but the sprinter has 10 seconds in which to pace out their objectives whereas the marathon runner has to work out how they are going to pace out the next 26 miles.

'What he's saying is that you need to think it all through rather than just go back. Well, after that, I do start to think.

'The first meeting with Bill is all about: "I will come and see you every month and we'll go through a few things and so on."

'So he's about to turn up, the first follow-up month, and everybody's in the office. One of the things that is troubling me is that the field managers are all behind with their field surveys and I say to him: "Bill, I have to tell you, the guys aren't up to date with their field surveys and all the rest of it."

'He says: "Well okay, they know their objectives, they know they've got to do that, ask them what are they going to do about retrieving the situation."

'Anyway, so the following month it's like, Oh My God, he's about to turn up, and I say to everybody in the office: "Budden's coming on Thursday, I don't want any of you in the office, I want you out doing the surveys because I'm not announcing that we're behind the plan, I don't want you in the office."

'So Bill turns up and there's me and the branch secretary and he says: "Where is everybody?"

'So I say: "Well they're all out working." He says: "Did they know I was coming?" So I reply: "Oh yeah, they knew you were coming but I sent them all out." He says: "Oh No! I want to see everybody, every month."

'Do you know what I say, this is London boy now: "Well you can't have it both ways, you can't see the people and you can't have your survey." He shoots back: "I want to see people, I want to relate to people."

'So the following month they ask me: "Mr Budden's coming, have we got to be in the office or have we got to be out the office?" 'So I say: "No, he wants to see everybody."

'So then he turns up, everybody's in the office. "How's everything, how are you Maurice, how are you Alan, how are you?" Then he says: "Right, let's go to the pub."

'We go down the pub in the lanes and I am agitated, I'm really agitated. I'm thinking well first off, in London we don't all go down the pub, especially during the day, and, second off, there we are in the pub drinking and drinking and I'm really getting uptight about it. Oh, and the other important thing is I'm still not living in a house, I'm still living in a hotel and obviously there are no mobile phones and the only communication to my wife is through a telephone box. 'So we're in the pub and of course after you've had a few drinks everything gets loosened up and then you've got other characters coming in, some of the field guys, and I'm thinking, hang on a second, these guys are all working behind the scenes, this was done deliberate!

'Now, not only am I having a drink with my boss, I'm having a drink with the field managers who work for me but they in turn have invited all the charge hands.

'So we're having a party. Well, come 2.30, the pubs would close. So I think, thank God for that, they're closing. The next thing I hear is: "Ah we're all going down to Marine Drive to the club there." I said: "What club's that?" "Oh we always go there with Bill," comes the reply.

'Oh My God! So, anyway, off we go and then come about 5.30 I'm just slaughtered aren't I? I can't do all this. I get on the phone to my wife and I remember the phone call all too clearly. "You're not going to believe this, Sue, we've been with the boss all day long drinking."

'She says: "You don't have to tell me, I can tell it in your voice," and she slams the phone down then and there! So I think to myself, I can't be doing this, I just can't do this every month. And the other thing was, I just couldn't afford to be doing it money-wise, let alone job-wise.

'So, I have to control things a little bit but I'm sure it is all stage-managed deliberately to get me to realise it's all about people and all the rest of it, and I have to say the camaraderie is phenomenal, it really is.

'Of course, I keep being very action-orientated – there's no question at all about that – but the amazing thing is, that in a short space of time, the branch results start to be incredible – really, really great.

'We are going way above plan and it coincides with Otis worldwide looking at the reasons behind customer cancellations, why they are cancelling contracts.

'The then CEO of the company, George David, whom we'll talk about much later, employs a management consultant, called Ken Myers, and Ken Myers is working with a whole bunch of people on going out, seeing customers, understanding: "Why did you cancel?", looking at all the data and trying to do some analysis.

'One of the things that he suggests is that Otis needs to get much, much closer to the customers and do some in-depth surveys with them.

'So, they propose to do this exercise in the UK and the one considered by the company as the most forward thinking of all the UK management, all the general managers that is, is none other than Bill Budden.

'So they approach Bill and say: "This is what we want to do, we want to get very, very close to the clients, we're going to do some customer interviews, that sort of thing, and we need to hone in on one of your branches." As I say, he has branches all over southern England, Plymouth, Southampton, Brighton, Southend and so on.

'He says: "You know what, we've got a young guy running

Otis HR director, Ken Myers seen as I am demonstrating Otis REM 2 to him in 1988. Ken was definitely charismatic and gave me my first insight to real marketing (4Ps). This, along with working with Barry Harden, who taught me all about segmentation, set me up to be a marketeer and not just a fancy umbrella and T-shirt dispenser.

Brighton, Bill, let's go and talk to him." So this guy Myers comes over from the States, we have a meeting, and it's Bill Budden's way – it is so clever – he's giving me a project that would probably stop me interfering with the day-to-day and managing the task. It's a clever manoeuvre by him but he doesn't realise actually where it's going to lead us, because it does lead us to greater things.

'Anyway, it's exciting because what happens is they say that we need somebody to actually go out and see the clients, and Ken Myers says it can't be an employee of the company: "We need somebody independent."

'Well Bill Budden knows this lady called Cathy Foster, and Cathy Foster is actually a former Olympic yachtswoman, because Bill is from Southampton. I don't know if he is a family friend or what but Cathy comes along and she is given the task of doing all the customer interviews and bringing back the feedback to me, Ken Myers and Bill Budden about what the clients are saying, what they think about us, and so on.

'So we start actually changing the way that we run the branch, not in reaction, but in taking on board the influence or the thoughts of the customer and saying, this is how we need to approach things.

'There is one simple thing…I always remember a client saying: "Well it's no wonder you take so much time to come and do a night call-out because I have to phone London for my night service." We said: "What do you mean you have to phone London for your night service?" He said: "When you 'phone through you get the answer-phone and it tells you to phone a London number."

'So what we do there is we introduce an 0800 number which dis-guises where the call is going, just to sort of give a different flow on things. Anyway, it works really well, and Bill keeps on saying: "How's Maurice, how's Alan?" He keeps on all the time, and he is at me all the time asking: "How are the people?" – not "How's the project going?"

'Anyway the project is going really well: the results are getting even better and then it is decided – this is how the powers that be work behind your scenes – that Otis wants to introduce for the first time into Europe this product called Remote Elevator Monitoring, REM.

'The history of REM is that back in the beginning of the 1980s, REM1 is introduced into the US and it's a device that can monitor the performance of a lift and, through the telephone lines, get hold of information about breakdowns and potential breakdowns.

'In the States, it's rejected by the unions because it is Big Brother, and bearing in mind we're talking about 1980-81, and the amount of data that is being produced is ridiculously cumbersome, not only do the unions reject it but so does the supervision, the field management, they just say: "This is crazy."

'So what they say is: "We need to have a different approach, a modified approach and the engineers are working on a simplified version of REM with better performance and quality." And they come up with what they call REM2.

'Then they say: "Well we need to find somewhere where we're going to pilot this thing. Ken Myers is at that time telling Otis that in order to reduce their cancellation rate, they need to industrialise the service. He knows about the innovation and work that is going on with REM2 and he says: "Look, there's only one place that you can pilot REM2 in the world and that is Brighton."

'So Otis decides to launch REM2, we are now talking about 1983-84, in Brighton, England – in front of the rest of the world.

'That puts me on a bit of a pedestal because, now, all of a sudden, I'm getting everybody looking at what's going on. But there's Bill Budden too who keeps on saying: "How's Maurice and how's Alan?"

'He keeps me right on my feet and he keeps on saying: "You need to think it through, you've got all these people coming here and you need to keep your feet on the ground, you can't put your head in the clouds and think that you've arrived. It just so happens your team have brought this around.' There is a couple of guys in the branch that I put on the project: Peter Chapman, Robin Crookes, and their careers take off as well.

'But it is an amazing experience and all of a sudden they say the

CEO, President of Otis, wants to come and see you and you just think, Holy Cow! So here I am, little branch office in the Lanes of Brighton, and George David, the biggest man in Otis, turns up on my doorstep.

'We offer him a cup of tea by the way, but he says: "No, I drink coffee, thank you." It is something else! When I think back on it, this whole introduction to people management comes from the Budden era. Then as things start to progress, I get nominated to go on my first ever proper management course which is run by a management college school called Harbridge House.

'It is an international programme and it's just pretty amazing because I've been nominated to attend this course in Evian on the French side of Lake Geneva. There I am with a whole bunch of international people, and I meet people that I, in later career, mix with again. But during that particular time, I start to learn a lot more about management, leadership and stuff like that. All this is sort of resonating in myself: hang on a second, I'm now on a different level in the organization, and it keeps on hitting me in the back of the head: your job's to manage people now, not manage the task. It is great to be learning some marketing tools and business planning tools too.

'During this Evian programme comes my first experience of corporate politics and it is actually really distasteful.

'The story is that we are on the programme for nearly a month, and at the end of it all we have to present a specific project that we'll work on back in our own countries and present it to one of the leaders of the various countries that would be attending the graduation.

'I am with three other English guys and we have to present to the MD of Otis UK.

'For one of the other English guys, his sole purpose of the presentation is to present how good he is to the MD, rather than how good the project and the collaboration and the learning are.

'Ken Myers is the first guy to introduce me to the four Ps of Marketing. I remember when we are working on our project, I say to the other guys we need to do an acid check on what we're doing and use the four Ps as the way to check what we're doing with our business plan.

'To which idea I get slammed, don't I? "That's a load of bollocks, you don't want to be doing that, this MD guy wants to hear this." I kept on thinking, do you know what, that's not right.

'Anyway, be as it is, I start to realise subsequently it is all about "me, me, me" with this character, not me, Bill Evans, but me, the other guy, and I think, I've got to be very careful here because that's not something I want to be involved in. It is an experience that isn't good, but there are several examples of politics that I have experienced throughout my career at Otis and every one of them is a memory which I've taken into D2E and I've said we will not have politics in this company because it is so counterproductive, it's so time consuming, and it's unethical. It's a lesson that I don't enjoy but it is my first experience.

'Returning to Brighton after this management course, the REM project is successful and we end up with 80 lifts being monitored. The branch results are great, we have great teamship. Then, all of a sudden, we have a bit of a commercial disaster, and that's when I meet up with this guy, John James, and we're going to talk about him in the next chapter.

'So my Brighton experience is all thanks to Bill. He is very inspirational and later in his career he comes out and almost uses me as his own mentor. It is incredible to think that I had looked up to him and then all of a sudden he isn't looking up to me but he is looking to me from the side. As I say, charismatic, incredible guy, people have always loved him because he always has time for them.

'When people meet each other and say "how are you" it's almost like you're a robot: "How are you", you don't really care, but you just say it anyway.

'When Bill says: "How are you?" he means it, "How are you?", and it is from his soul. So yeah, I really, really enjoy that time there. It goes like a rocket in time and believe it or not, within just over two years, due to all the recognition, due to all the success, I am then invited to go and work in Otis headquarters in London, and take up a new role as the marketing manager for the company.

'But what a transition! Here's a man of action trying to sell the best lift systems in the world and now learning that his job now as a manager is all about managing people, it's all about thinking things through. You don't have to look busy by carrying stuff, you are busy when you're thinking. That's all down to Bill.'

Genuinely care about the people you work
with. In a management function, your
focus should be on the people, rather than
on the tasks.

• • •

Think before you act. Thinking is
also working.

• • •

Give people the space and responsibility to
reach objectives in their unique way. Avoid
micromanagement. Don't tell them what to
do; ask how they would reach the objective.

• • •

Motivate people with an individual approach,
learning opportunities, inspiring colleagues/
managers, enough autonomy and a balance
between work and play.

• • •

Keep your feet on the ground, including when
things are going well.

• • •

Avoid corporate politics in your team,
it's counterproductive, time consuming
and unethical.

So You Think You're Superman

CHAPTER FIVE

It's the critical moment in the vital game. At just 20, Bill Evans is captain of the second team of Old Strandians. It's a lot of responsibility for him to carry – not to mention extra leg work – in such a strong team. He's playing at Left Wing, and he and his old schoolmates are now surging through the rain sodden, wind-swept semi-finals of the London Old Boys Cup.

Getting there hasn't been easy; they've made it through stiff opposition from the likes of Tiffins, Alleynians (Dulwich College) and Latimer Old Boys.

Ten minutes from the final whistle to a fast-paced away game, the score stands at 2–2. The result is too close to call. Then, just as the Old Strandians are making a final push, there's a foul inside the box: Bill's team is awarded a penalty. This could be the decider.

Heart pounding, Bill has no doubts as to what he needs to do next. As he readies himself, one of his young team-mates, Roger, trots up to him: 'I'll take the penalty, Bill,' he says. But Bill is in no mood for diversions from his intention: 'No, Roger, no,' he says, 'I'm the captain, I need to take this penalty.' Two more team-mates chip in quickly: 'No, let Roger do it!' Bill overrules them: 'Look, I have to take the responsibility here.'

So, overcoming all doubts – and any lingering objections – Bill carefully places the ball on the spot.

He decides to angle his shot past the goalkeeper – off to the left. Bill's right boot connects well enough with the heavy leather ball and off it thuds towards the goal. But, as if in slow motion, he sees, to his dismay, that the ball isn't swinging quite wide enough. It's not much of a stretch for the goalie to gather it in to his right.

It is a scene that Bill will have plenty of time to remember – and relive – for the rest of his days. The match is lost. There will be no final. It's a silent journey home. Nobody from the team wants to speak to him. 'I feel like shit,' recollects Bill.

Now, a few years later, Bill is running another high-performance team down in Brighton, this time for Otis. It is just after the company has launched its transformative REM (Remote Elevator Monitoring) Mark II.

Following on from the marketing initiatives launched by Ken Myers, Bill is keen to put together a major internal communication event with the full workforce at the branch present – around 40 people all told.

Bill picks up the story: 'So there I am, organising a meeting in a hotel for all these people and it is actually very unique for one branch to have a big, full-blown meeting like that in a hotel for a whole day, because you can imagine you're closing down your customer service in the field. So, it is quite a bold step to take.

'Anyway, Johnny James gets to hear about what I am doing because it was in training – that is his role as the training manager.

'Now, Johnny is probably just over 50 years of age at this stage, he is a small man and one thing about John is that he is constantly smiling. When he walks through the door into the office, when he says: "Hello!" he says it with an incredibly warm smile.

'You know some people, when they talk, they're always talking as though they're laughing, and he is infectious – you just feel so comfortable with the guy and he is a joy to work with.

'Johnny used to be a construction manager working for Otis but he's now been recognised as someone that is a very caring, bloody experienced and knowledgeable guy. By this time, he's been singled out by the company to lead the apprenticeship scheme throughout Otis UK.

'Bearing in mind the apprenticeships are five years long in those days, he has a whole army of apprentices he has to look after. But his home town is Brighton, so he uses the Brighton office as his base and that's how I get to know him so well.

'"Bill," smiles Johnny, "do you need any help with your big

meeting?" I say: "Well I don't know, you know." In truth, I am not too sure what on earth I am doing with such a big event but I do say to him: "Well, yeah, I may do." So, he says: "Okay, well give me a shout if you need any help because you've not done anything like this before." I say: "Okay."

'Now, all the apprentices look up to Johnny James and he has considerable success with them going on to become fitters. Indeed, he helps me later on to interview for sales trainees and he is always looking out for one of his boys who have been apprentices: "We're moving their career on," he explains. So, he is always looking for people to develop; he is one of these people who take pride in seeing people flourish – an incredible attribute really. A lot of people in corporate life want to see people getting on but they don't want to see them really getting on above them. Johnny isn't one of them.'

The day of the big meeting draws near.

'Johnny says to me: "How are you getting on with the preparation for your meeting?" So I say: "Yeah, we're going to go through all we've been doing with the Cathy Foster customer feedback interviews, then we're going to go through what we're doing with REM2, and finally, we're going to run through how we're going to change some things to improve the customer service and all the rest of it.

'He says: "Right, so, who's doing all of this?" So I say: "Johnny, I am." He comes right back at me: "So you're think you're superman, then?" I reply: "What do you mean by that?" He says: "So you're going to do the fucking lot yourself?" I say: "Well, yeah, Johnny, that's how it works, I'm the branch manager. I've got to show leadership." Quick as a flash he says: "You've got it all wrong, mate. You really have got it all wrong." He says: "Your job is to facilitate and to help people to flourish. You've got really good field managers in Maurice and Alan Day, you've got a really good sales guy, you've got really good administrators. Why don't you delegate to all these people a different section of what's going on? That way you get buy-in."

This time, Bill heeds the well-meant warning. "'Okay." I say.'

Following Johnny James' firm guidance, the Brighton branch office goes on to have a highly successful internal communication away day. But the learning does not stop there for Bill. As a branch manager of a small team, he has just discovered that the most important priority was not to manage, but to lead.

Another, more formal, and more visible, challenge to his old habits comes soon enough.

By the time Bill moves back to working in London as a service director, the company has decided to embark on a training programme through an organisation called Coverdale. Coverdale's founder, the legendary Ralph Coverdale, is rated a business genius by none other than John Harvey-Jones. An ex-army officer, Coverdale has read psychology at St Catherine's College, Oxford, under Bernard Babbington Smith who specialises in the nature of human perception.

Bill recalls the sheer impact that the Coverdale training makes on him.

'In the army you give a command and people dutifully go off and perform the command. But what Coverdale realises is that they would do the command regardless of why they were doing it or what they were trying to achieve.

'He develops this process for getting tasks done. It's actually quite a simple template whereby when you issue a task, let's call that an objective, the most important thing is to actually state the purpose; why are you trying to do what you're trying to do.

'Oftentimes people go off – and, let's say you've been told to go and paint a post red – off they go and paint the posts red and the whole purpose behind it is that is supposed to be a warning to people not to walk into the post!

'So, if you tell them the purpose first then they may say, well, hold on, why are you painting it red, really you should paint it yellow. But because you don't explain the purpose, people don't do the task as well. Then, even more importantly, when you give out the task, you're also supposed to say I want you to do the task by five o'clock this afternoon – and I want the paint to be dry.

Superman. Is it a man, is it a bird? No, it's Bill Evans. It's not too much of an exaggeration to say there was a time I really thought I was Superman but, after I got a critical penalty decision completely wrong, the lads on my team soon taught me I wasn't. Artist Maramgoni has done well to capture the extent of my youthful illusion!

'So you must also give them the end result!

'Part of the Coverdale process is all about making sure that you've got a systematic approach to getting things done. The smart thing about it is that once you've done your task, the process demands that you actually review the success criteria.

'So, in other words, if you say that you want it to be red by five o'clock and you want it dry, then if at half past five the paint's still wet, what do we need to do to improve our performance?

'So, anyway, off I go with my team in the London service department to have our education sessions with Coverdale. Our coach is this great guy called Joe Hindmarsh. So here we are given the task of building a tower out of spaghetti. Not cooked spaghetti, uncooked spaghetti. We are given a few things to do to help that; some string and other bits and pieces. So, Joe says: "I want you to build a tower and you've got 30 minutes to do it. Off you go."

'So here I am with my group and I'm busily tying up bits of spaghetti – and tying up this and doing that – and we erect the tower and we're nearly at the 30-minute mark and then, guess what, the tower falls down! Result: we've got no tower and a load of broken spaghetti all over the table.

'Joe takes me to one side, because part of the Coverdale thing is it also involves one-on-one coaching to the task leader, and he says to me: "Bill, I know you're the director in charge of all these people, but you're not supposed to do all the work." He says: "If you look at what you've done, you haven't bothered to think about it, you haven't delegated to everybody. It seems to me that you have this obsession that, because you're the boss, you want to do everything." He said: "You need to stop and think."

'So here we are, we've got the football example, we've got the Brighton example, and now we've got the spaghetti example of me thinking I'm bloody superman – and the whole thing has just got to stop.

'What Coverdale did for me was a life changer. The change was kicked off because Johnny had originally said: "So you want to be Superman" but what Coverdale did was to give me this framework that constantly reverts back to the basic: what's the purpose, what's the purpose?'Further on in my career, I start to work closely with Robin Cheeseright at D2E, and Robin was particularly good at being a coach. He would sit down with people and say: "Now, what are we trying to achieve? You're going off to a meeting: what is the purpose of the meeting, what are you trying to achieve?" Robin would actually spend a lot of time preparing people and building up their confidence, so that they would go off and excel at what they were doing.

'Robin was an expert. He could do it all himself but he saw his role as a leader to be a coach, which is dead in line with all the things that I mentioned about Coverdale and all the things that I was not yet doing.

'One of the most important things about being a leader is that you don't have to do it all yourself, you don't have to be the expert, your job is to motivate the team, to be the conduit, to be the facilitator and so on.

'When I finally do come to that realisation, a lot of things really start to get better for me. And when I become the marketing director on the executive at Otis, I begin to have a whole team of people working for me who are actually better than me.

'We have Felicity Stonehill, a highly trained communications professional, we have Erin Brau, a really top class educated lady from the US, we have Elspeth Vaughn, who again, was highly educated, we have Chris Bowler who was a chartered engineer, we have Derek Smith, one of the best technical directors in the lift industry.

'I look around at all these people. All of a sudden I think, do you know what, they're all better than me but they all look to me to be the leader. So I start to realise, that the whole idea of what you do as a leader is to motivate your team, hire better people than you.

'It's not about telling people: you've got to be subordinate to me, you know. If you don't have a great team, you're not a great person and the better your team, the better you are, not the other way round!

'So, from that point on, I begin to share with my team their successes and take pride in what they are achieving and always look to ensure that people are reaching their fullest potential. I stand back and I look at their success and privately share that success.

'As I move even further forward, I start to realise that, okay, I've come up with great ideas and I am an ideas person. I am an innovator and all the rest of it, but now I come across a tool that is part of the Six Sigma quality tools. They call this the KJ-method or KJ Technique after the Japanese human psychologist guy, Jiro Kawakita, who actually worked on the development of the "affinity process."

'You're greater than the number of people in the team if you apply what they now know as the KJ method. The KJ method gives everybody in the team an opportunity to input to the task, but the fantastic thing about it is that the process is done in silence.

'So everybody uses post-its and there're lots of descriptive items and lots of picture diagrams that you can see in the KJ method. But what it's doing is enabling people that aren't usually so prominent in a team meeting. You will always get the loudest vessel, but sometimes he's the most empty! What KJ does is to bring everybody an opportunity to input to what you're trying to achieve as a team or as a business.

'What I have discovered is that if you take the Coverdale training: here's the task, here's the purpose, this is what we're trying to achieve – with its systematic approach of saying what has to be done by when and by whom, and then apply the KJ method inside that process, you get the most fantastic team dynamic.

'Out pop all the ideas and you haven't just got a spokesman for the team because everyone is forced to input. Great stuff comes from it, there's no two ways about it.

'We use this systematic approach at D2E today, it is a phenomenally strong weapon. We use it at the beginning of all our action plans. When we started with the subject of sustainability we wanted everybody to input and we got everybody in D2E all working on the same page. Everybody is using the KJ method to come up with the action plan which ultimately forces us into: here's our vision, here's our strategy, here's our action plan. This was all done through the KJ method.

'That brings me onto another angle to this topic. When you've got a team, the most important thing is that you have a team of people that are representative of your client-base.

'To me that is true diversity.

'It is all about having a balanced team that represents your client-base, and if you don't have a diverse team you will never have a broad enough approach to your strategy. Why is that? Because you're back with the superman scenario when superman thinks it is all about "me".

'But you could also experience exactly the same problem more generally in sector group-think. 'Oh, so you men over there, you think you know everything, you don't need somebody that represents a different gender, in your team composition? Meanwhile your client-base, certainly in the property sector, is dominated by fantastic women in senior roles, executive roles.

'So it could be that you're being blind to the whole issue of being blind.

'Above all, diversity is a sound business principle. That's why you should have a diverse team which is fully representative of the market. It should not just be because you're going to get a high ESG rating or top marks in Wall Street for having, for instance, enough women on your board.

'Twenty or 30 years back when Jack Welch was CEO of GE he wrote a great book about his time in leadership. I read the whole book because I was holed up in a hospital with acute diverticulitis. My Otis colleague, Tuch Sherane, came in to see me in hospital and he brings me the book, saying: "Get your teeth into this."

'I'll be honest with you, I did read it all which was pretty rare for me. One of the things that Jack Walsh did, it was during the era of .com, was to take on a mentor of 17 years of age who was a geek. This person went to see him two hours a week on a Friday afternoon and took him through all the latest gizmos on the web.

'So, here you've got this massively strong leader and he finds a 17 year old can teach him more than his IT VP. I have adopted exactly the same approach because I say to all the youngsters in my company: "You have to challenge everything we do because if you don't we're not going to move forward."

'You know, social media is so strong these days, I haven't got a clue about Instagram, Twitter, TikTok and all the other platforms… Facebook. I mean I don't know how they all work and there're so many things to keep up with. How are you expected to know how they all work? Don't forget LinkedIn is the business medium at the moment.

'The whole point about it is that if you want to have a dynamic company and move forward, you simply cannot say: "when I was here, what we used to do is this, this and this," you have to allow for the fact that new people, young people, diverse people, are essential to a business flourishing, because otherwise you're back to the superman scenario: "I know better".

'The reality is, as a leader, you don't know better, but what you do know is these people can make, if you like, the whole machine better together, and you need all this diversity. You need these people to have the opportunity of input, you can use tools like KJ for sure. You can also use the Robin Cheeseright scenario: let's talk about what you're trying to achieve, how you're going to do it, give me your ideas, let's sleep on it overnight and then let's go forward.'I wanted to be superman when I was captain of the football team, I didn't want the best guy to take the penalty.

'I had to learn the hard way.'

Don't let your ego stand in the way of what
you could accomplish as a team if you would
let or help the people around you flourish
and outshine you. The better the people you
surround yourself with, the better you are.

• • •

Don't try to do everything yourself;
stop, think, delegate.

• • •

As a manager, your main job is to help people
flourish and reach their potential. Prepare, build
confidence, coach, motivate, facilitate.

• • •

When giving a task, state the purpose, the
end-time and the (clearly measurable) desired
result ("What are we trying to achieve? By
when?"). It gives employees the chance to come
up with better solutions, and they will do the
task better because they understand the purpose
and get a sense of responsibility and autonomy.

• • •

Use methods to get input from everyone
in your team (also the shy and silent ones),
and make sure you have a diverse team that
represents your client base. You need diverse
input to avoid being blind to your own
blind spots.

Basically

CHAPTER SIX

The man who stands at Bill Budden's club bar in Brighton is all of 16 stone and over 6 foot tall. But it's not his strong build – or the fact that the drinks are flowing freely from, to and around him – that marks him out.

Everyone seems to gravitate towards him, hang on his words, seek his approval, and want to share in his confidences. Pulled by a personal magnetism, there's something about him that Brighton branch manager Bill Evans knows is powerful. And that he wants on his side.

'Basically...' the man continues, as he launches into another piece of worldly wisdom to his workmates.

The man in question, Micky Burrell, is, like Bill, a South Londoner. He is a gear man in the repair team in Brighton, having come to Otis after an apprenticeship in a fabricating business.

Bill's first reaction is: 'What the hell is the man doing at the bar? He should be working!'

'When he first walks in, he ignores me, not because he disrespects me, but his focus just isn't on me. Up he goes, straight to the bar, and immediately wants to buy everybody a drink.

'Everybody is clamouring round him and I think to myself, this guy's a pretty influential fellow in amongst all these other workers. I am fascinated by him, and I think to myself, well that's one person I've got to crack in terms of changing the way that we work down here because he is clearly influential.'One of the things that is most amusing about him is that virtually every sentence starts with "basically." We all say these things, especially me, we have these pet phrases, and you don't realise you're saying it, but Micky is saying "basically this, and basically that."

When I get to know him better, I realise, without him knowing it, every time he is saying "basically" he is looking at

'Sound as a pound' Micky Burrell, was another South London geezer. Micky became a great personal friend of mine and Sue's. We were to spend a lot of time with his family. He had an unbeatable line in banter, loved football, was a great golfer, and ended up as captain of the Littlehampton Golf Club. He was finally even accepted by the establishment, inside Otis and beyond.

things from a basic point of view, both his feet on the ground.

'So it's almost as if the way he speaks is reinforcing the way he thinks, you know, this "basically" thing. A while later I am looking at how we are going to change the way we do the business. How we can get the show on the road and get some productivity going. I just start thinking and I see that this Micky Burrell, well, if I don't crack him, I'm not going to crack any of them. 'So I invite him into the office and I say: "Micky, you come from south London, I come from south London, we've both been working on the tools, we've got a lot in common. I understand you love football. I love football.

'"But one of the things I need you to do is help me change the way of working down here because we've had the guys moonlighting. Some of the business is being lost because the performance isn't good, the productivity is low," and I say to him: "I want to make you a chargehand."

'Micky looks at me. He says: "You're having a laugh, aren't you?" So I said: "No, no Mick you're a leader and I need you on my side and I want to make you chargehand."

'Immediately, Micky asks: "How much more, how much more am I going to be paid?" So I say: "Well, you get, I forget now, but you'll get a chargehand's allowance." So he says: "Okay fine."

'So off we go, and it starts. He is now part of the success criteria. But there are a lot of things about Micky that you can learn from, and we have one situation where one of the fellows, his guy, has finished the job and in those days it is classic issue: it is a work practice called "job and finish," so they'd go and do the job and then go home.

'Of course, some jobs are quicker than others: if they could do it quick enough they could go home early. That is definitely the culture of Brighton in those days – so you couldn't criticise the individuals because that's how they are all working.

'Anyway, so this young lad does the job, finishes up and goes home. The client contacts me and says: "I can't believe your mechanic's done the job. He's left at two o'clock and you've charged me a full day's work and I'm not going to pay you." So I say: "Well, okay, let me look into this." Anyway, my first thought is, we've got to stop this because the tail's wagging the dog.

'So I call Micky into the office and I say: "Look, Mick, we can't carry on like this, the guys are just running riot. I'm going to have to take a stand." He says to me: "Well, what are you going to do?" I say: "Well, I've got no alternative. The guy has falsified his timesheets, we can't have that. Unfortunately, we've got to sack him." To which he says: "Are you kidding me?" So I say: "No, I'm deadly serious. I said we've got to stop this."

'He says: "you can't do that, he's a good boy. I brought him up, I've taught him everything I know. He's only done what we've all done." I say: "Yeah, I know, but somewhere along the line you've got to stop it." So he says to me: "You're not showing any sensitivity to these people." So I say: "Well okay, in which case I'm going to have to deal with it my way but at the end of it all we've got to change." So he says: "Okay what are you going to do?"

'So I call out this young lad in the office and I go into my office, he comes into my office and I say: "Now sit down, young man." I say: "You're really lucky because Micky Burrell is protecting you from getting the sack." I say: "At the end of the day, you do what you've done again and you're out. You need to go and thank Micky for keeping you in the job."

'I earn a lot of brownie points that day by doing that because Micky says: "Thanks for giving him a bollocking, he knows he's been stupid, he shouldn't have done what he did and all the rest of it." At the same time, I gain respect from Micky as well as from the guy.

'It starts to tell me that as a leader you do really have to look at the basics and the sensitivity of leadership. So that leads me, some time later on, to probably one of the best leadership books ever written. It's by a guy called Ken Blanchard and the book's called *The One Minute Manager*. It's one of these books you can read in probably an hour and a half and it's full of quick blast comments such as "catch somebody doing something right." So often, managers and leaders say: "you did that wrong," and it's almost like the mother shouting at the child:

1970s Brighton. Looking back on my career, Brighton ranks near the very top when it comes to enjoyment and success. We achieved so much, indeed we notched up quite a few industry firsts here. I even went to the Goldstone football stadium, then the home ground of Brighton & Hove Albion. Can you believe that – for a Crystal Palace supporter – inside the home section of our fiercest rival?

"Johnny stop doing that, Johnny stop doing this, Johnny stop doing that."

'Well poor old Johnny doesn't know what he should be doing, all he knows is every time he does something, he's told he can't do it. 'We often focus on leadership in a negative way. What *The One Minute Manager* teaches us is that you should be all about identifying good practice and giving what he calls a one-minute praising to not make a big issue about it three weeks later because you missed the opportunity, but give somebody praise when you're actually catching them doing something right.

'The other thing is subtlety. When we say "well done", what value is there in the "well done"? Usually there's not a lot of value because you hear "well done" all the time. What he says is if you actually touch somebody on their shoulder and say "well done", you're actually connecting through a sensitivity channel.

'It's a fascinating response because if you do that it's almost back to when you're in your family, when you hug people it means a lot, lot more. Obviously, you can't go round hugging your workforce too much but you can put your hand on their shoulder and say, well done, you really did a great job there, thank you very much.' So, *The One Minute Manager* is actually endorsing this sensitivity thing and then of course you come on to the bigger subject of when you talk about emotional intelligence. There's been so much written about it but it's all about understanding the sensitivity of people, whether it be your workforce or your customers or your colleagues. Emotional intelligence is something that usually you can't teach too well.

'Some of the people, certainly in our book, have got emotional intelligence and they can use their sixth sense to their advantage. Oftentimes you push back on your sixth sense and just say, yeah could be, could not be, I'm not too sure...

'The smart person says, do you know what, my sixth sense is telling me something, and this is where the entrepreneur usually has got the knack for saying, do you know what, if we go and do that, I reckon this will happen. The worst thing of all is not to use your sixth sense and then you come out with the statement "if only" and "if only" is really the pits.

'So back on Micky, Micky with his football expertise. He's a natural team-builder and sees the strengths of everybody. He personally supports West Ham but he is extremely knowledgeable about the coaching side and in fact one of his very good friends, was Bobby Houghton the coach manager of the Malmö team that nearly won the European cup.

'One of the things about any team sport is actually the word "team" and you don't really appreciate the word "team" until you actually analyse it. There're loads of different examples but, sticking with Micky for the minute; you're running a football team and you've got 11 players, and each one of the players as an individual has certain skills and attributes that you've got to blend into the 11 people.

'So, you have your defenders, your midfield, and your attackers, and they all have to work cohesively together in order for the team to win the game. If they don't work together, they can still be individually fantastic but the team's no longer cohesive and they'll lose the game.

'When I am fortunate enough to be at the IMD in Switzerland on an executive programme, one of the things that we do is we look at the differences of what they call "groups" of people versus "teams" of people.

'You could have a football team where they're full of individuals, they're not a team, they're just a group of players playing on the same pitch. Where you have a team in which they're all working hard for each other – that's when you know you have a team. So, the definition of team is when the unit is actually working cohesively in the same direction.

'One of the first things that we do at the IMD is we actually analyse the film of Apollo 13. Apollo 13 is a true story about Neil Armstrong and all his colleagues on a spacecraft facing disaster. You've got a group of people there and, to start with, they are all full of ego, well certainly the film really focuses on their egos. They're all pulling in different directions. It isn't until they start to realise that, hang on a second, unless we pull together we're all going to die here.'Armstrong is able to get them all to, you know, delegate his stuff: "You do this, you do this here, I've got to do that," and so on and: "We've all got to work together otherwise we're going to die."'The interesting thing there is they are forced into being a team and so often teams are only formed when you reach a breakpoint. You can often have a business situation where unless we go and do x, y and z we're not going to have a business anymore or unless we put a roof on the top of the house we're all going to get bloody wet. 'When circumstance forces you into doing something, you're more inclined to do it. This is the moment where the leader starts to actually earn his keep because you don't really want to be saying: well, when's the next disaster because if I get a disaster coming along I can make them into a team. Do you see what I mean? You don't want that!

'What you do want is to say: right, I've got a group of people here and I need them to work as a team, so, who's strong in this particular regard and who's not strong in another particular regard?'You can go straight back to the football scenario of course where you can see this guy's good in the air, this guy's good at tackling, this guy's good at dribbling, you can identify the strengths of the individuals to put them into positions such that they can work as a team. 'If you're in a business environment sometimes you can't actually say that person is perfectly suited to do that particular function versus the person doing a different function. So, the example here might be: would you ask your accountant to do your marketing plan? Would you ask your engineer to go and do the sales pitch? 'You know the bleeding obvious, but it's when you get down to the finessing that you need to look at even deeper attributes.

'One of the available tools comes from another one of these industrial scientists called Belbin, where the focus is on personality types and how they fit into the team.

'In a business context, you could have the person who's best at taking all of the notes and following up with the actions, somebody who's best at innovating, another who's best at scheduling or chairing the meeting.

'By the way, just because you're the boss doesn't mean to say that you're particularly good at chairing a meeting! You could just be a participant and allow somebody else to flow the meeting. So, when you come back to looking at the football team, is the football captain the best player on the pitch? The answer is usually no, he's not. 'The football captain is actually the best leader. The misconception is that people get promoted because they're really good at something and then you put them into a position – up to a point of incompetence – which is not really fair. So you have to study people in so many regards.

'This is why I like Micky Burrell because: "Basically," he would say, "Darren was stupid, but he's a good guy, he's really good at gear work and all the rest of it, and, yeah, he was stupid but give the guy a chance." So this is life down on the ground, not big leader territory where I want to show my muscle, where I've got to sack somebody to make myself look famous.

'When you see somebody doing something good you should say well done, you should put your hand on their shoulder. This is the sort of stuff that is the emotional intelligence that we need to possess but usually it's the people like Micky Burrell that think the basics are far, far better than the high-flying CEO.

'The CEO sits in his ivory tower with all the wonderful furniture around him that's cost an absolute fortune and is wasting a load of corporate money. At the end of the day, when it comes to actually making the whole machine work, you need Micky Burrell.

'Here's another thing about Micky: he has a very high ethic. 'Interestingly when he gets to learn about the guys moonlighting he says: "They're stealing from us." He is one of the guys that comes along and he says it is about time someone did something about this.

'The ref in a football match can go up to a player and say: no more tackles like that because if you do you're going to get a yellow card.

'This is how you should look at it from a business point of view. 'I don't know if it's a good example but at the moment we have the

Home Secretary (Suella Braverman). She's inadvertently used her phone and email account in a way that has breached security. So, she's fallen on her sword and resigned. The Prime Minister Rishi Sunak has then said: "But you're a promising Home Secretary, so I'm going to give you a second chance."

'We do not know how that appointment will turn out. There's a political storm about the security and all the rest of it but from a Rishi point of view, he's saying because it's a basic error we've got to give the person another chance here.

'He's sticking his neck out big time. There's no textbook to say in this circumstance you should do this and in this other circumstance you should do that.

'For sure everybody in a regular job has a contract of employment and it says: "Thou shalt not do this, that and the other." But it doesn't talk about the day-to-day management of things like that, does it? If you spell a word wrong, are you going to get the sack? No, but you should expect somebody to come along and say, by the way, that needs correcting.

'It's about getting the balance right. This is why I like Micky so much because he seems to have the talent to deal with all of these things and yet "all he is," and I say that not in a derisory way, "all he is" is a gear man from south London but he has something about him that nobody else is prepared to take on.

'I think, to be honest with you, the previous managers are frightened of him because he actually has so much influence over the workforce. But what they don't do is say, hang on a second, I can use that to my advantage, which I do.

'After I leave Brighton, people start to realise how important he is in terms of influence and capability. Customers love him, he becomes a field manager and then ultimately an account manager in southeast England.

'And from a guy that used to walk around with dirty work clothes, purely because of the nature of his job, not because he is untidy, he becomes Micky Burrell the boss guy. Yeah, he gets smartly dressed and always wears a suit, a tie and a top pocket handkerchief.

'As I say with the other influences in this book, it's all about when he walks through the door everybody says: "Oh it's Micky Burrell," and they all want to talk to him.

'Micky has the foresight to say: "I don't want to live in London," it's not where he wants to bring up his family and that's why he has moved down to Brighton. He's a very proud, very family orientated guy but the love of his life, apart from his family, is football.

'He becomes a personal friend, our families get together. Micky is a guy that I really like.

'Unfortunately Micky dies prematurely with a kidney infection. It is really sad because he is so loved.

'He's been the captain of the golf club down in Littlehampton. 'At his wake at the golf club you can't fit all the people in because there are so many who want to go there and pay their respects.'

If you want to have an influence on your employees, look at who they already naturally respect and are influenced by. Don't be afraid of an employee with a lot of influence, use this to your advantage.

• • •

When an employee does something wrong, there's often no textbook answer for the situation. Find a balance between the right correction and basic human sensitivity. Don't just show power, but also look at what a person needs, and at what a person can mean for the company. This helps all parties to gain respect for one another.

• • •

Catch them doing things right, IN the moment (not later). Shift your focus from the negative to the positive. Use subtlety in your praise – a shoulder touch will help you connect through a sensitivity channel.

Having and using emotional intelligence is an advantage, but it is hard to teach. It's about understanding the sensitivity of people and about trusting your intuition to move fast when it feels "right" (So you don't end up with "if only" statements).

• • •

There's an art to bringing a team together:
Look at your team as a sports team. Look at everyone's strengths and weaknesses and blend these into a team.
You can look at their functions, but also at their personality types.

• • •

There's a difference between a group of individuals, and a team. The latter cohesively works together in the same direction, and for each other.

• • •

The strongest teams are formed when things are at stake and a situation or circumstances force a group to become a team.

Walk the Job

CHAPTER SEVEN

Success depends upon previous preparation, and without such preparation there is sure to be failure – Confucius

It is a show down alright. The two Otis representatives have been summoned to a critical meeting on site at the world-famous Dorchester Hotel with the main director of one of their biggest customers, international contractor, McAlpines.

There's no time for small talk. The director is plainly not happy. He wades straight into the two executives. This in 1990, explains Bill, in the days when all construction contracts were adversarial.

Soon the director is shouting at the top of his voice: 'Otis haven't done this, Otis doesn't do that, Otis haven't done…'

Inside the hut room, the senior Otis executive bides his time patiently. A baleful stare is the only clue as to what comes next.

All of a sudden, a huge pair of hands smash down on the makeshift table – not much more than a plank of wood balanced on a trestle. The top flies up into the air, together with all the site plans.

In the stunned silence that follows, the Otis boss looks at his customer straight in the eye and says: 'You haven't got a fucking clue what you're talking about.'

I first meet Roy Markham when I'm a supervisor. He has just been appointed as Otis' London service manager.

'Up until that point, he's had a very colourful career at Otis. And even while still an apprentice, he was a superstar. He's gone out to Uganda and done a lift installation over there single-handed with local labour. He's even met Idi Amin so that's the sort of stuff he's got up to.

'Roy has also been out working in Japan and in Paris. It's in Paris that's he's met his wife, Heidi, who is German.

'So when he arrives in London service, he'd travelled all over with

Otis, and later Schindler, director, Roy Markham was very proud of his upbringing in Brixton. I went to school there too, and we found we had so much in common, not only as South Londoners but as workplace comrades. When we were on safari in his beloved South Africa, we had some real-life adventures – and we talked nonstop! I miss him: boss, friend, mentor, mate.

Otis and just before this job he has been a construction manager for southern England. There he is, a young guy who's just four years older than me and takes over. Immediately you can see that this guy has got something.

'The first thing you notice about Roy is that he has hands as big as banana bunches. I mean his hands are enormous. Everyone would say: "My god I wouldn't want to get on the end of that!"

'He is a colourful character alright and we all get to like him pretty much immediately. He is an incredible contrast to the previous guy. He is very warm and empathetic to all the field people because that's where he comes from.

'Now Roy and I seem to strike up a pretty good relationship and our origins are not dissimilar. He is born and bred in Brixton, and he is proud of the fact that he comes from South London, even though he's had international experience from Japan and Paris. I went to school in Brixton too. So, Roy Markham, Bill Evans and David Bowie: we've all got the same backgrounds.

'Anyway, early doors one day, he comes along and clearly things do need sorting out in the Otis London service operations. So, he decides, which is quite amazing, to interview everybody for their jobs. We all think, well hold on, this is a bit bizarre.

'He goes through the process of talking to everybody and asks: "What do you want?" and all the rest of it. Then he says: "Right, I'm reorganising." He creates three divisions within London, City West and South and so I get called in and he says: "We're moving you over to the City."

'Well, I'll be honest with you, I am really devastated because by this time I am loving working in the West End of London, Park Lane, Mayfair, Soho – you name it, and to be told to go over to the City is a bit of a knockback for me. Having said that, on reflection, it turns out to be probably one of the best things ever – because it starts to broaden my perspective.

'Anyway, so I am working away over in the City and it comes to the point where I have to go to Brighton (and Roy is instrumental in that move too, by the way). In the meantime Roy has been the director of the factory in Liverpool for a while and then, several years later, around 1985 or 1986, he is put in charge of all the Otis London operations.

'I always remember him saying to me: "So what are you doing?" By this time I've been made marketing manager for the service business, so I say: "I'm in service marketing." He says: "That's no job!" So I say: "Well yeah, it's important." He says: "No, you're better than that." So he makes me area service director for half of London. At that time the job entailed all of the business other than new construction and new sales. So I have pretty much everything.

'It's around then that Otis wins the Canary Wharf project: it is just a phenomenal success to win that contract and so the whole of the company's attention is on Canary Wharf. In my operations team we're looking after servicing, repairs, modernising lifts and indeed replacing them.

'We have also won the contract to replace all the lifts and put two escalators into the Dorchester Hotel. It's a project that is well beyond my capability at that time, a really big and important one, but not as important as Canary Wharf.

'I'm now stuck in charge of this thing and Robert McAlpine are the main contractors that are doing the complete fit out of the hotel, which has been recently bought by the Sultan of Brunei's investment company. They are spending absolute fortunes on the place.

'Part of the design involves running two escalators from the kitchens to the dining room – to deliver the food – which everybody thinks is unheard of. So here I am thinking, shit! How are we going to get these escalators into the building? I'm worrying and worrying – because I simply don't have the experience.

'Anyway, as I fear, the project starts to go horribly wrong and so I say to Roy, who is my boss, I say: "Roy we've got a problem down with McAlpine's, this is off and this, this and this." So he says: "Right well we'll go and see them."

'Just prior to the on-site meeting with McAlpine I have been in hospital for a cartilage operation following an accident that I have had skiing while I am on the management course out in Evian. I've had the operation, come out of hospital and the following day I've got to go to this meeting at the Dorchester Hotel with Roy. The evening of the site visit I am also off to see Eric Clapton play at the Royal Albert Hall. So, it's all happening!

'So Roy says to me: "What time's the meeting?" So I say: "We've got to meet this guy at 10.30." He says: "Right, I'll see you there at 8 o'clock." So I say: "8 o'clock?" He says: "Yeah, we're going to walk the site." I look at him and he says to me: "You don't go to a meeting unless you've got all your facts." He says: "We're going to walk the site, we've got 20 odd lifts, we've got two escalators." He says: "I want to see every single one of those before we go into the meeting, so we know what we're talking about."

'So this is a top example of being prepared. You don't go to a meeting unless you've got all your facts and his solution to that meeting challenge is physical fact finding: "I want to see it for myself."

'We walk around the site and we're clambering over the roof top machine rooms and my knee with the cartilage is starting to swell up because they have warned me to take it easy – so I am in a little bit of agony there. Then we go into the famous meeting with the McAlpines and Roy's big banana hands come crashing down wallop! on the table.

'So the bloke says: "There's no need to be like that, Roy."

'Roy says: "Listen, we've listened to all your shit, I have been 'round every single one of these lifts, there isn't one lift shaft that's ready, you've got lift shafts full of water and you're telling us that we're running late."

'He says: "You haven't even got lift shafts for us to do the work. So he says: "Go and do your own preparation before you come to a meeting and, when you're ready, we'll come back." He says: "Come on Bill, we're going."

'I'm scampering to go: "Fucking hell!" I'm thinking, Oh my God, this is how you do these projects! We go out and he puts his arm on my shoulder and he says: "That shows 'em. Know what you're talking about before you go to a meeting."

'So I always remember that and I preach the same lesson about it all the time. Alright, sometimes you don't do as much prep as you should do but I have to say that was the perfect example of being able to confront an adversarial situation by knowing the facts. So that's what I have learnt from Roy, but I've learned a lot, lot more.

'Roy does some really great things in his career. The one that should not be forgotten is the way that he turns the remuneration of the field force around to being one based on integrity and honesty. He convinces the hierarchy of Otis that the old way of paying people in the UK a living wage, by them doing a ridiculous number of hours of overtime is all wrong. People are booking overtime but not working it, and he convinces the unions, the management and the hierarchy of Otis that there has to be a fairer way of working.

'He introduces a thing called the Working Partnership.

'That is where people are paid more or less a portion of their overtime which is put back into their hourly rates and people go on to monthly pay. It's Roy's revolution. The unions think it is a fantastic idea, they go along with it, they recognise that we cannot carry on the way we are, in the industry.

'The union pulls away from the main industry union and decide to have the relationship directly with Otis. This particular initiative epitomises, to me, what Roy is all about. That is someone that truly believes in integrity. He is an honest man and he expects honesty in return. You can swear at him and say things that you wouldn't want to put into print, and he would take it all. But never call him a liar because if you called him a liar he would blow his top.

'I remember on one occasion in union negotiations, someone there suggests he is not being quite straight with them. Whack! The bananas come down on the table then and it is the second time I see them actually at work. It is just amazing! He says: "Listen, everything I tell you is coming from my heart and from my brain and I'm not manufacturing anything, don't ever, ever, ever accuse me of not being straight."

'I just think, you know, he is a man to be admired.

'He goes on to become a legend in the industry. Unfortunately later on in his career he falls foul of corporate politics and so he ends up leaving Otis and joining Schindler. But he is the guy that leads the negotiation for Otis to buy Express Lifts.

'Typically, when he is doing the deal, he stands in front of the whole of the Express Lift company workforce, explains what is happening, takes on a leadership of magnitude and people admire the guy for the way that he deals with everything.

'His meticulous preparation for union negotiations, for the purchasing negotiations of Express Lifts and his ability to stay concentrated through that process is admirable.

'It wasn't until many years later that I realise that he's probably learnt quite a bit about preparation from his time working in Japan. 'I too find myself learning how to truly prepare when I am in Japan for three years in the early 2000s, responsible for product strategy. When they are working on engineering projects, I can see the meticulous care and attention the Japanese have when they prepare for a product launch, with all the engineering, marketing and the sheer amount of holistic input to whatever they do. We all know that the quality of Japanese products is second to none. So I think possibly Roy has learned a lot from that.

'The other thing about Roy is that, after his spell in the Liverpool factory and return to London as the overall director, he is appointed the managing director out in South Africa. He does some marvellous things out there, including gelling the multi-racial workforce together. Then he comes back to Otis UK to become the overall commercial director. One of the things that he does when he gets back is a similar thing to what he did before: "Right, I'm interviewing you for the job you're doing."

'Once again, he decides to restructure. He wants three positions to report to him. One is the service operations, the other is the new equipment operations and the other one is the sales and marketing operations. But, here's the catch: there are four people and only three jobs.

'I remember going away to the RAC club in Epsom and we do a lot of talking about strategy and stuff like that and then he says: "Right I want to talk to each of the four of you." So the other three guys, who are in a similar senior position, and me, we are all interviewed and Roy says to me: "So, what job do you want?"

'I remember saying to him: "Well probably I'm going to be the unlucky one out the four." He says: "Well, why's that?" I say: "Well I'm the newest one to the bunch and the other three have probably got more experience than me." He says: "Regardless of that, what job do you want?" So I say: "I know service very well, I've been doing marketing very well so either one of those two jobs would be fine." He says: "Well I think you're a bit more sales orientated than the other three." So I say: "I'll be happy to get a job." Then he announces the judgment. He calls me in and he says: "Right I'm making you executive director of sales and marketing."

'I'll be honest with you, I am taken aback. I am over the moon at getting that job. At the time I don't particularly care who has the other two jobs but the loser in the four is the guy that I never imagined would be the loser and Roy moves him out.

'So I start working alongside Roy as sales and marketing executive director, and that's when we really start to change the shape of the company and start to grow. We grow the sales business, and we move the profitability up too.

'One of the other things that Roy does, and I use it even now, is that every single Monday morning we would talk about the negotiations we have going on: what preparations do we have to put in place, what do we need to do to win the job, who's going to do this and who's going to do that? So, we have a war room meeting every single Monday so the whole of the company is aligned for success. There is no individualism about this, it's all about teamwork and who is best placed to win the job. That in itself is something that I take with me.

'After he leaves Schindler, he decides on early retirement. He's fallen in love with South Africa from his days there and he subsequently buys a lodge on a game farm.

'He invites Sue and I out there to go there on safari and we have a wonderful time. My War Stories probably start then and there, because he and I just laugh continuously. We are chased by herds of elephants on more than one occasion and go out stalking lions. I'm talking about serious adventure stuff.

'One day his jeep breaks down in the middle of an area half the size of Wales and it is just the three of us, Sue, Roy and me. The jeep has conked out, and he and I are outside the vehicle and we're saying to each other: you mustn't move more than a metre away from the perimeter of the jeep otherwise the animals would see that as a threat. We just laugh. It is a memorable relationship.

'When Roy eventually passes away with cancer, I am privileged to be the person to organise his memorial service and I'll always remember, he calls me up to the Cromwell Road Hospital and he says: "Right I'm giving you £10,000 and I want you to organise a celebration of my life at the RAC in Pall Mall."

'With the family, we organise this massive celebration of life. There are people queuing up to be invited, but we are limited to the 150 capacity. He is a legend and I owe him a lot. What do I learn most of all from him?

'Well, firstly his honesty. His integrity stands out but his work method of always being prepared (it's almost like the Boy Scout thing: "Be prepared!"), was I suppose the thing that I have learned most from him from a working point of view. That's what I carry with me.

'When I start to do my role over in Otis World Headquarters, and I travel around the globe – and I do travel a hell of a lot – one of the things that I try to do by way of preparation is to understand the culture which I was going to.

'So I use *The Economist Information Unit* to get some degree of understanding about the country I'm in – how big's the GDP and how many people live in a particular city, and all of that. I make sure I am always being able to drop something into a conversation so that they know that I have a level of care about who I'm dealing with. It pays dividends, but the dividends really come from the amount of preparation beforehand. It takes a broader spectrum than just that.

'Around the year 2000, when I am in Singapore on a $90 million subway contract negotiation, I find I have to go every single month

Henry Dunbar, joint founder of Dunbar and Boardman, was christened Little Legs by Roy Markham. Henry grew their lift consultancy to be the market leader, until D2E came along. Henry was old-school, and the way he conducted business reinforced my determination to make D2E independent, impartial, transparent and ethical. Thanks, Henry.

for just one meeting on a Friday afternoon at four o'clock. A 22-23 hour journey for a two hour meeting on a Friday afternoon! We're unable to change the time of the meeting; that's the way they are, the Singaporeans are precise. Their attention to detail and their project negotiation is just incredible. These guys start to come into a meeting with shopping trollies full of all the files relevant to the thing they are discussing. They meticulously take notes, writing down every detail of all the questions and all the answers, and circulate detailed minutes of meetings and all the rest of it.

'As I say, you can't go to the next meeting without reading the previous minutes, you have to prepare, you have to prepare otherwise you'll be laughed out of court for not having the competency and the integrity that you need to do your business. One of the things that I learn is when I eventually get involved in the Otis University – a fantastic initiative by the company to have development programmes within the company itself, because Otis is large enough to be able to do that.

'Soon I find I myself as one of the first people to join the board of directors of the Otis University in Europe and subsequently, as the company centralises, that moves over to the States. When I am in World Headquarters, I am on the board of directors there and then I became chairman of the university.

'One of the preparation exercises is about the power in the question and not in the answer. It is a lot of fun. So, part of your preparation to go to a meeting is working out what questions are you going to ask because, if you're not armed with questions, you're not going to find out anything.

'We are doing this exercise amongst the very senior leadership of Otis Europe, my great friend Marco Bonnisonne and Bruno Grob, we are all in this training thing together and it is all about the power of questions. We are given the subject and we have to write five questions about it that we are going to raise with the expert or the client, or our colleagues. We write the five questions down and then the rest of the people in the group score the questions based on their power.

'For a start, how much does your question make the other person think? If you just ask, "What's the colour of the wall?" You might get "White!" Well, they haven't had to think about that much, because they can see it. But if you ask a much broader question like, "Why did your architect put the wall here?" then they'll have to think a bit more. Not only that, but you'll get more information out of them. So that's what I mean by a power question.

'So now, when it comes to going to a meeting with a client, I always say: "Okay, part of your preparation is what are the five big questions you're going to ask?" This is all part and parcel of getting your prep.

'It could be you're going to go to a meeting and the client's going to build the tallest building in the world. Well, we know that's his objective but what's the strategy behind the building? So, one of the greatest questions of all is: "Can you elaborate on the strategy for your development?" Then you just sit back and listen – it's amazing what you can find out.

'During all the sales training in my time at Otis UK, including sales management training from Steve Jessop, the talk is about funnelling. Funnelling is the big question you ask at the top of the conversation, and then you filter, filter and filter down. That's all part and parcel of the same subject: preparation.

'So, you don't go to a meeting and start thinking: now, what shall I ask him? You don't do it like that. You go to the meeting prepared, and part of that has to be: what are the big questions? Now let's go back to the Dorchester Hotel, here we are preparing for the meeting, so what are the big questions?

'Okay well, the big questions, there are: "Let's have a look at the job site, let's see what's going on in the broader progress of the project, what's the situation with interface trades, who's preventing us from doing our job?" So you're constantly questioning everything that's going on, not just the myopic: what's in front of me? It's back to Roy Standen, "taking a wider view;" if you take a bigger view, you've got more preparation. So that's what it's all about."

LITTLE LEGS

'One of the things that Roy wants to do in our days running the commercial operations is to get closer to the lift consultants, because the lift consultants are seen as, if you like, not a threat, but we are worried about the ethics of their role.

'Roy says: "Right, let's call in the key lift consultants and actually share our strategy with them and ask them what their strategy is." So here we are, we've got this consultancy and the leading one is run by both Peter Boardman and Henry Dunbar (Now TUV Dunbar Boardman).

'Peter is the intellect, Henry the driver. Henry's a bald guy and Roy would be very basic: he would do stuff that you're not allowed to do today. I mean he would go up to people, smack them on the chops and say: "Hello scungy boy, how're you doing today?"

'If you were "in" with Roy, you actually got: "Scungy bollocks", "Hey you, scungy bollocks!" But if you don't get the "bollocks", it means you are down a peg and if you don't get "scungy" at all, you are really down a peg.

'Roy would come up with descriptions of people, as I say, you couldn't do it today, but anyway, he refers to Henry as "Little Legs", "Fucking Little Legs here and Fucking Little Legs there."

'So anyway, I've got to prepare a presentation to give to these blokes about our strategy, and so I prepare a fancy PowerPoint presentation and, as you know, you have to give the file a name. So I saved the file as "Little Legs." Seeing as it's internal, nobody's going to be any the wiser.

'So here we are the boardroom and I'm booting up my computer, so of course it boots it up with the desktop in full view, and I've got to click on this file called Little Legs and of course everybody in the boardroom sees, including Henry and Peter, that the file's called Little Legs.

'Of course, Roy and a couple of the others start laughing their heads off and of course then the question comes from Peter and Henry: "What's so funny?"

'Roy just says: "Oh, that's just Bill, he's come up with some stupid name for a file, why on earth he's called it Little Legs, fuck knows." It was because of him!

COLLAR BONE

'You know another thing about Roy's popularity, when he is being treated in the Cromwell Hospital for cancer the hospital tells me he's got more visitors than George Best.

'I arrive there because he's summoned me to give me this instruction to organise his celebration of life. I am pretty conscious of not saying: "How are you?" to someone in his state. A week or two earlier I asked: "How are you?" and he's turned round and said, "I'm fucking dying, aren't I!"

'So I went in there and I've just put my hand on his shoulder and said: "How's it going?"

'Later I go down the pub with Joan, his partner, and then I come back to the ward and I walk in and everybody's laughing, including Vanessa, his daughter. Roys says: "Do you realise what you done?" So I say: "No."

'"You broke my fucking collar bone!" I was devastated so I say: "How did I do that?"

'Roy says: "The way you bashed me on the shoulder!" Of course, the cancer has got into the bones and he is so frail with only a few days to go.

'Anyway, Roy says I will have to shoulder him: "Right," he says, "You can be one of the pallbearers."

Good preparation prevents bad performance.
Meticulous care, preparation and eye for detail
lead to higher quality (as seen in and done in
Asia). Be prepared.

• • •

Make sure you have all the facts
(and go see for yourself).

• • •

Prepare the right (big) questions and work out
how you will funnel down to filter out the
right information.

• • •

Understand the culture of the people you'll be
working with; show you care.

• • •

Get clear on your aim.

Prepare with your team, so you have the right people on the right tasks (this is motivating as well; together "in battle").

• • •

Read all the details from the last meetings, so you're up to date.

• • •

Regularly check if employees are still happy and positively challenged; and if you can't put them in a better position to benefit the company, have conversations about this and restructure accordingly.

Integrity and honesty are important.
Continuously strive for a fair way of working
(Money, diversity, working hours...).

• • •

A devastating turn might be the exact thing
you needed, in hindsight.

• • •

At the end of someone's life, celebrate them
rather than mourn them.

Two Ears One Mouth

CHAPTER EIGHT

It is back in 1979, the year of the Iranian Revolution and the Soviet invasion of Afghanistan. Donna Summer is singing about *Bad Girls*, Chic is thumping out *Le Fric* and Art Garfunkel is crooning through *Bright Eyes*. Bill is now 29.

Alongside other colleagues, he has been sent on one of his first management courses by his new boss Roy Markham. The team is learning by role-play. Split into groups, class members have to pretend to be either the union rep, the manager or the mechanic.

The communications skills course leader is telling them that even if they can talk very fast, say, at 170 words a minute, they can hear or process at least double that.

Pint-sized Otis stalwart, Charlie Morley, who makes up for his size by ruling his City team with an iron fist, commanding management respect into the bargain, puts his hand up: 'Listen, I don't get what you're saying. How come you can hear twice the amount you speak?'

A large man at the back of the room, in his 50s, turns round and deadpans him: 'Charlie, you've got two fucking ears and only one mouth. It's simple.'

For several minutes members of the course cannot contain themselves

"I'd been supervising a little while in the West End of London, in Soho and Mayfair, for the Hilton Hotel and customers like that. 'Then Roy Markham comes along as the General Manager for London. There's a reorganisation and he wants to shake things up. So he moves me over to the City.

'I find myself working in EC3 and EC4, where we have prestigious buildings like Commercial Union, Kleinwort Benson, Barings Bank, the Baltic Exchange, prior to the bombing, and also the original Lloyds of London.

'I am invited, along with a whole bunch of other supervisors in London, following Roy Markham's reorganisation, to go on the famous supervisors' man management course.

'Bear in mind this is my first ever formal education in management or leadership and we go just outside of Crawley to a small business school.

'We're going through all the basic information about motivation and it's the first time I've heard about Maslow and his hierarchy of needs.

'A lot of this stuff, I'll be honest with you, is going right over my head. The process they use is role-playing..

'To this day I'm not too sure what we are trying to achieve really but it is a hell of a lot of fun, and helping Roy Markham through the process is Bill Budden, and the training manager, Alan Seddon, who orchestrates the whole scenario.

'Well, the rest goes down in history. Once the comment is made, the place comes to a standstill for ten minutes. We just cannot stop laughing. First, we can't get over the fact anyone actually speaks to Charlie like that. Second, it's the brutal way he delivers the fact: "You've got two ears and you've only got one mouth, simple!"

'And the name of the legendary big fellow is Bill Davis. Bill is an escalator supervisor and his claim to fame is he is the construction supervisor up in Liverpool when Otis are installing escalators up there.

'They'd take the mickey out of him because it just seemed like every time he put a pair of trousers on, the trousers were having a "trial separation" from his ankles.

'People would joke: "What's wrong with your ankles – don't they like your trousers, Bill?" We'd to laugh but he'd to thrive on it. Once people get a recognition for something, if they're an outward personality, they're always going to lap it up and I'm sure that he'd deliberately wear trousers that were too short just to draw attention.

'He was a lovely London character and he had a brother working at Otis as well. For ever more he will go down in fame as being the man with two ears and one mouth – and the way he came out with that put-down in the middle of a training course.

'But here is the serious point: it really is a cornerstone when you're in a leadership role that the whole idea is to listen and take in what's going on. Not to overrule or to try to command the whole of the meeting with your talking. If you do that, you're missing the trick.

'So, this "two ears and one mouth" thing, even though it was terribly basic at the time – and gave us all a good laugh – I've actually taken that mantra to heart many a time and said to folks: "You're not listening!"

'Which brings me on to the other old favourite: are you hearing or are you listening? That's a fundamental. So many times people are actually just gagging to speak, waiting to interrupt. They're not listening because they're sitting on their agenda, and so this question: "are you hearing or are you listening?" is important.

'Back to two ears and one mouth. The two ears you've got are for real listening, not just for receiving noise. If you look at the whole aspect of listening, there's a skill there that you can only develop if you actually understand body language.

'I can't remember exactly where I first learnt about body language, but we had this Australian guy called Dr Joseph Braysich, who was a lecturer on the subject. There are so many people today who talk about body language but the body language fundamentals – it doesn't matter who the lecturer is – are all the same, because body language is a universal human language.

'One of the things that I did learn early on is about people touching their mouth. When people are doing that when you're talking to them, it means they're not listening because all they want to do is: "I want to talk, I want to talk!"

'It's a throwback to when you are a kid; you are back in school and you're putting your hand up, "Miss, Miss I need to say something!" "Miss, Miss I want to go the toilet." So, you're not listening to anything because your hand is actually saying: "I've stopped listening, I want to talk!"

'Body language is vital, it doesn't really matter if you're a salesperson, a manager, or a CEO, you need to read the body language to understand whether people are listening. More to the point, you need to control your own body language to demonstrate that you are listening. So yeah, the fundamentals of body language become very, very important in the leadership tool kit.

'This is where we find we have a dilemma now with modern technology. As I have said earlier in this book, when you go to a meeting, one of the ways that you can use to demonstrate that you're listening is by taking notes.

'So first you establish courtesy by asking: "Do you mind if I take notes?" and then you're taking notes and they see: "Oh, he's receiving me" and at the end of all your notes you just say: "Can I just confirm my points?" That's all the proof you need to show that you've listened.

'Of course now, more frustratingly, people don't actually walk around with notebooks. These days you'll find that people are using their tablets or their iPhones. They're automatically putting notes of conversations directly onto their phones and what with the phones and the tablets being small, they're now putting a barrier up between themselves and the client.

'"I hope you don't mind I'm taking notes" may be the best they will come up with. But they're not really asking for anybody's permission, they're just telling the client what they're doing. Personally, I don't buy that way of doing things as good enough – just turning on the phone and putting the dictator on. I think that is particularly rude – but that's how the world is going.

'Getting back to the more fundamental point of listening, this is a skill that really has to be developed. I think some people may have it naturally, but I don't think it's second nature for leaders. Quite often, leaders are extrovert and what comes with that is they talk a lot. If you are a wise leader, you should switch from "talk a lot" to "listen a lot". In other words, you are going to have to turn 180 degrees away from what comes naturally to you.

'Often you have to pull someone up in order to help them learn the skill. The other day in my company, one of the guys turns 'round to another person and says: "Will you please stop talking and listen to us!" We all smile because we're at such a level of trust and comraderie that he is able to say that.

'The other bloke replies: "Yeah I know, I know, I can't stop it, I can't stop it!" Then he stops talking and he's sitting there with his finger on his mouth, like: "I have to stop talking but I still want to," because he's got his finger on his mouth.

His body language is yelling: "I want to talk!" The body language is actually fighting with his efforts to sit still, so we've got these two things going on at the same time: "I want to talk and I've got to shut up, so I'll just put my finger over my mouth." It's quite funny.

'So now you know that he's not actually listening at all, he's in a dilemma: "I've been told not to talk but I know I've got to say something." You wouldn't know this is going on if you don't know anything about body language. A manager should always try to get some basic skills in body language.

'I'm also amused by some of the tell-tale signs of people exaggerating – when they're talking and they're rubbing their nose. I'm not quite sure how this sixth sense of the body works on the person who's telling the story, who's exaggerating or, even worse, telling lies, but there they are, they're rubbing their nose.

'Apparently, the hairs inside the nose start itching when you're doing that. When you take a lie detector test, how does the lie detector work? Well, it's obviously picking up some signal coming off your body but every single one of us has got an in-built lie detector in the hairs of our noses.

'So when people are talking and they're rubbing their nose, you know damn well that they're not actually giving you the full story. Of course, if you're listening and observing the body language you can detect these things rather than just relying on hearing.

'Another skill that helps you to listen better is having the ability to ask big questions. The bigger the question, the more power is in the question. But if you are asking a powerful question, please do listen to the answer.

'It's all very well having a smart question but you're not going to get anything out of it unless you're prepared to listen to the response.

Dave, my great friend for over 50 years, wanted to book his own place in this book. Here's Dave showing some basic body language signs. Top left, a barrier: Dave doesn't like you. Top right, Dave rubbing his nose: he's exaggerating or even lying. Bottom left, Dave's thinking. Bottom right, Dave wants to speak and he's not listening to you.

There is a skill in developing your questions and going to a meeting and being prepared with the big questions and then shutting up and letting the two ears do for the one mouth.

'Long after the supervisor training, at a Great Marlborough Street development scheme, just along the road from Liberty, I am invited to go along to the principals' meeting. Now, principals' meetings for any new development are usually very long and sometimes quite tedious. It all depends on who's running the show. At this particular development, the property development director of a very well-known company proved to be a total professional.

'He was so good at it we all went along willingly to the principals' meeting – more because of him rather than because it was a project requirement. So, I'm sitting there and they're talking about the toilets and they're talking about this and that. You will appreciate lifts are just one small aspect of a building, even if they are a strategic element, they're just one aspect.

'Anyway, the main conversation is between the development director and the architect because it is a challenging building. It is on a tight, existing site in Soho and there are lots of different implications behind that. One of the key ones is waste removal.

'So the meeting gets onto the subject of waste removal and I'm just sitting there and thinking... nothing to do with me, lifts and all the rest of it... but I am nevertheless, listening hard. To be honest with you, sometimes I get very tired at the end of the day because I feel I've been listening too hard, you know.

'At a certain point I hear the client say to the architect: "Okay, now walk me through the waste strategy." So the architect says: "Well, as you know, in the City of Westminster, they have waste collection daily and so the euro bins will be placed on the pavement at 10 o'clock in the morning to pick them up." So the director says: "Oh right, great, so we've got that sorted."

'He says then: "Where are the euro bins?" The architect replies: "The waste is stored down in the basement in the euro bins." "Oh right," says the director, "how are the euro bins going to get up to street?" So the architect says: "They'll come in through the lifts."

'Now if I haven't been listening at that point we would be missing a really critical thing. So I pipe up: "How big are these euro bins?" The architect's team say: "Well they're the standard euro bins." I say: "Well what's the dimension of a euro bin?"

'They soon tell me and I say: "Well, we've got a problem." They say: "What's that?" I say: "Those bins won't go into the lifts, they're bigger than the lifts that we can put in the building." The developer says to the architect: "Now you've got a problem." The architect says: "Well we'll have to make the lifts bigger." The developer then says: "How are you going to make the lifts bigger because we are using the existing lift shafts and you can't do it."

'The whole of the project comes to a standstill because they can't move the waste out of the building because they intend to use euro bins which are standard for the waste trucks to pick up. You can't just use a smaller-sized bin because the collection carts won't be able to pick them up and flip them into the back.

'The development director says: "Well, you better go away and work out how you're going to change your waste collection." The whole point there is if I had been switched off I would have missed that point and it was fundamental to that project.

'You know what the interesting thing is: I don't know if it's to do with the waste or not, but that project never goes ahead. It starts to get too complicated for their needs. The viability of the building becomes less and less.

'So, as I say, you could be commanding a meeting or you could be just a participant in a meeting. It's really tough to be sitting there and listening when sometimes it's not directed at you but, as I say, it's all part and parcel of the job.

'On a positive note, nature gives us these wonderful tools – the ears – and it's part of our five senses system, isn't it, to listen. The more you listen, the more opportunity you create for yourself. In fact, if you're listening hard you can hear clients start to deviate in their conversation and, if you're taking any notice, you may be able to say to yourself: "Hang on, there's an angle there."

'You can also look at it from an internal perspective, such as in a staff meeting. If you are doing your job, and listening hard to what people are saying, you can also pick up employee satisfaction or dissatisfaction.

'One of the things that we've been doing at D2E over the last couple of years is having what we call a "pulse meeting" with every individual.

'Personally, I love it because I go along with three questions, three big questions, and then I say: "Right listen, the gloves are off, you can say whatever you like, tell me how you feel about the company, tell me how you feel about this, this is not an appraisal, this is not a review, this is me listening to what you've got to say."

'I've passed on that task and that approach to the two directors of the company and they've done it this year and they have found out a lot, and also I think they've enjoyed it as well. I think other companies do that too but it's probably quite difficult to do it if your company's really big. Once you get bigger you can do sampling and things like that, the word gets around.

'I think it's great to listen to things. When you think about how much of our leisure time is spent listening to the TV, or the radio, or music, if we were to take a little bit of what we do in our private life into our business life, maybe business might actually be a little bit more enjoyable.

'How many times have you come away from a meeting thinking: "They didn't listen to us" and it's probably because they were talking too much. "They switched me off!" You can soon tell if people are not listening when they start looking at their watch, that's another body signal, simple thing, they're looking at their watch, a slight little glance down at the watch, you're boring me. But if they're talking they won't look at their watch.

'Within Otis, I think certainly Roy Markham was a great listener. Although that's almost a contradiction because we all used to listen to him, because he was such a smart guy. He used to take on board what you would say, there's no question about that for me.

'Other good listeners were over in the States, where I found that my experience was being listened to, well certainly on the lifts and escalators side. I'm not so sure about when you got into business strategy things – I think that they always thought they knew better. Probably they did.

'But I think that Sandy Diehl, who was my boss when I went over to being VP in the States, had the ability to ask some really big questions. He would draw things out of people: "Well, what do we all think?", draw them out and listen to them.

'I mean he was a very intelligent, very educated guy running a very diverse group of people in product strategy. We had a German guy, an Italian guy, a French guy, an English guy, an Indian guy, and a couple of Americans.

'One particular time, he called in a psychologist because in strategy, you really do have to think. So, we were in the boardroom, Otis World Headquarters, and this lady came in and she had this porcelain egg, a big egg, and you could only speak when you were holding the egg.

'So, if you weren't holding the egg you just had to listen.

'It was an amazing exercise and it's almost the same as the KJ method where you eliminate speaking altogether. The KJ method doesn't require you to listen but I suppose the final point I want to make is you can be really, really effective by not talking at all.

'I suppose the umbrella concept is to listen and observe. I guess that is really where I'm at with the body language; making sure you're actually on "switched to receive."

'I'm fascinated by some people that are incredibly good at listening – so good in fact that you start to think, I wonder what they're thinking?'So you start to get deeper and deeper...You only really find out what they're thinking by asking them a question. And here again you should never ask people what they think, you should ask them what they feel.

'"How do you feel about that?" It's just a small difference in the question but you get a much fuller response.'

Listen (don't just 'hear') and show that you listen to people.

• • •

Take notes (but ask for their permission first, don't just announce).
Summarise their points to them when they finish talking.
Avoid phones or tablets – they create a barrier.

• • •

Use tools like the KJ method or a talking stick/egg to make sure everyone is heard.

• • •

Listening is incredibly effective, especially in a leadership role.
You can pick up details that make ALL the difference.
You spot opportunities.
You pick up (dis)satisfaction in employees and clients (= angles and opportunities).

• • •

Also listen when you are not involved or the topic has nothing to do with your responsibilities; it's always possible that you bump into valuable information.

Reading others' body language and controlling your own, can be a very valuable tool. Observe if others are listening and show that you are listening.

• • •

Touching mouth: they actually want to talk, they are waiting to share their own agenda.
Rubbing nose: they are exaggerating or lying.
Looking at their watch: they are not really listening or interested.

• • •

Have personal conversations with your staff (we call them "Pulse Meetings" at D2E).

• • •

Make them feel comfortable enough to open up and be honest.
Ask big questions that push people into giving a lot of information.
Ask 'How do you feel about this?' rather than 'What do you think about this?' This way, you get a fuller response.
If the company is too big, with too many employees to ask individually, use proper sampling.

Drop Your Pants

CHAPTER NINE

The neat figure with the tightly cropped hair and glasses takes up his position at the lectern in Otis's state of the art factory. It's the early 1990s. Fifty or so Otis keen salesmen have assembled to hear him hold forth on value propositions in the conference room.

With quiet deliberation, the presenter folds his notes, sets up the presentation deck, puts his agenda up on screen – and opens his mouth to speak.

'Before I start,' says the man, looking Otis UK's top commercial director in the eye, 'Bill's told me to drop my pants.' And before anyone can say another word, or move a muscle, a pair of freshly laundered Y fronts hits the deck.

The salesforce stares at the presenter in disbelief and they begin to look at one another – totally mystified.

So, Bill recalls: 'Let me describe Steve Jessop and then I'll tell you how I first met him.

'Steve Jessop is a professional sales management educator with his own company. He's got a great track record and, without a shadow of a doubt, he walks the talk and practises what he preaches.

'The other fascinating thing for me is that he's a Virgo. One of the main characteristics about Virgos is that they're perfectionists – and they're never wrong. It's interesting because I'm a Virgo and Virgos actually like each other according to the astrologists.

'Funnily enough, Sandy Dichl is also a Virgo, that's why I get on so well with him. But Steve is very particular, he's always dressed smartly, he always carries his briefcase, he's always very well prepared.

'One of the things he tends to ask is: "How many pens have you got in your briefcase, because you need to make sure you've got two that work, not one." He always prepares thoroughly for meetings, everything. He's a highly precise, very organised guy.

'So I first meet Steve in 1993 shortly after Otis UK is restructured and I am given the role of Sales and Marketing Director by Roy Markham.

'I can't actually claim the credit for Steve walking into Otis, indeed he's already reached out to John Baker and managed to persuade him that he should meet the other directors and pitch for work with Otis and, what's more, convince Otis that we desperately need help.

'By this time we still have John Baker and Lindsay Harvey in their respective executive roles, along with myself, Trevor Perry and Roy Markham who is, by this time, the commercial director, having returned from South Africa.

'Anyway Steve's pitch is straightforward. It's: "I don't know if you need help, but in order to identify where you've got gaps in your sales processes, in your whole management pipeline, in your whole management of business development, I recommend that we do an audit."

'His proposal is to spend time out in the field with the salespeople, doing joint meetings with clients, seeing how they operate, looking at the quotation process, the follow-up process – the whole sales cycle – and that's part of the audit.

'Now, at the time, we aren't doing too bad as a company. And, of course, I'm mighty proud because, remember, I'm a Virgo as well, so I think everything's perfect! Steve goes about his business and after two or three weeks of audit he comes back and he presents the report.

'Basically, he says: "You're crap!" and I've got to be honest, I was pissed off. "We can't be that bad!" "Well you are!" "No, Steve come on, we're market leader." He says: "I have to tell you in my estimation your whole sales organisation is out of control. They're giving away the products, you're not making any money."

'Well, he is absolutely right. It turns out we are selling new equipment at almost zero margin and we have, at the time, around £30-35 million's worth of new equipment sales. So that's the situation, because the business idea then is that you sell the new equipment and you make your money on the maintenance. That is the psychology, anyway.

'So he tells us we're crap. I suppose, because I am much younger then, I actually am upset as well as annoyed and it takes me two or three days because I am now thinking, I'm in charge and he's not only said that the sales organisation is crap but, hold on, who's in charge? I am! So I suppose the criticism is pointed straight at me. Having said that, I've only been responsible for the sales organisation for a short period of time, less than a year.

'Anyway, so I say: "Okay let's sit down, let's have a conversation." Well at the time he says to me: "One of the biggest problems is that you've got two sales managers: one in London and one outside of London, and it's impossible for them to manage the sales force because they have got too many people, there's no process management, nothing of the sort."

'Now, one of the things that Steve Jessop advocates, or his business advocates, is that sales training per se is actually a waste of money. That is quite a position statement because his approach is that in order for the sales organisation to change its habits and its processes, it has to be managed from the top all the way down.

'So the ownership of the change has to start at the top, rather than saying: "Fred, John, Peter you go off on a sales training course and you come back, and now, because you've been on a sales training course you can sell better." He says that doesn't work. So his whole philosophy is, you have to start from the top.

'"Well, okay," I say: "We get that, so we have to start from the top, but the only problem is we haven't got an infrastructure to actually manage the sales force, we only have these two guys." So he says: "Look you've got a lot of sales guys here, and you need to break down the regions."

'So the first thing that I do, with his encouragement, is to appoint five sales managers; one in Ireland, one in the North, one in the Midlands, one in London and one for Major Projects. So now I've got these five sales managers, by the way, one of them was Robin Cheeseright, who ultimately comes over to me at D2E, and Steve says: "Right, I will work with these guys and we will develop sales management practices for Otis."

'So we start working with Steve and one of the things that he emphasises is that, as a sales manager, you don't manage history, in other words, you don't manage the results. So if you declare: "We sold 10 lifts last week." Well, that's not managing, that's just reporting data. What he says is that the job of the sales manager is to manage the activity.

'If you want to sell 10 lifts, what is your success ratio? Well, we might say, 1 in 3, so that means you need to do 30 quotes to sell 10 lifts. How many visits do you need to make to the clients in order to get the quotes? Well, maybe 2 or 3, so, let's say 2. You need to make 60 visits. How many phone calls do you need to make before you get the visit? Let's say 2, so that's 120 phone calls.

'So you work your way back to the origination of the activity and you manage that activity. He calls it "the boot", so you look at the funnel and then you look at the outcome – and so on. All of a sudden, we go to creating proactive sales calls and that's what we soon introduce formally.

'Now the interesting thing is, the other guy that I've often spoken about and see as a guru is Daniel Priestly, who's written many books – and he will always give you a useful quote. One of them is: "It's all about the leads." If you aren't creating leads, you're not going to create a quote, and if you're not creating a quote, you won't get an order. So what we do back then is pretty fundamental. We emphasise the management of the activity, we create a booklet and a sales management practice binder.

'At that time I always have, on a Friday afternoon, a copy of the sales managers' teams' diary commitments for the following week faxed to my office. I don't always read it but they think I'm reading it, they think I might come along, whatever.

'From that time on, we are all about the sales managers owning their team and Steve is constantly pushing: "You have to own the team." He creates training for the sales managers like the joint-visit protocol which is a fantastic exercise in itself. He would also ask:

Steve Jessop is a 'walk-the-talk' sales practitioner like no other. While he may have a terrible choice of underpants, he has proved that humility can win an audience over. I have stayed in close touch and called upon his counsel for over 30 years. Yes, 30 years.

"How do you do the follow-up?" "How do you do the review?" "Have you actually understood what the client wants?"

'One of the tools that Steve reveals is all about funnelling. You go from the five big questions and funnel down till you actually get the client to say: "Yeah give me a quote, I want to go with you."

'So all of these things are constantly being dinned into the sales managers' heads and, in turn, they have to train and, what's more, follow-up with their people.

'It is remarkable because, over a short period of time, maybe two years, the sales of the UK company, the order intake, starts to really grow like topsy. If I can just give you the timeframe from 1993 to 1997, when I go off to the States, we've gone from £35 million to £90 million and zero margin to a positive 15% margin – a huge improvement.

'Categorically, it could never happen without Steve's direction. 'So, at the end of the day I end up being the hero, this is what I have done, we've pushed prices, we've reviewed prices every quarter, we pushed them by 1% which is a story that I take with me further along the track when I go over to the States. All these sorts of things were gold-dust, but I think the most important thing that Steve emphasises to everybody is about value.

'As soon as you start sharing and giving information to a client, Steve says you're giving value. You need to get commitment back. As a salesperson you can give away products for promotion which is a Priestly-ism but at the end of the day you need to get commitment. When you're starting to give advice don't give the crown jewels away and then say: "Well, I've told him everything and he hasn't come back to me." The reason is you haven't got commitment.

'So Steve does a lot of training on value propositions to make sure that you're not giving it all away on Day One. Always make sure you have the commitment first, as in: "If you're interested in improving your business and you want to see some more profits we've got tools that can help you."

'"Really?" "Yeah." "When you're interested, I can come and

meet you." "Oh, can't you tell me over the phone?" "No, no it's much better for me to meet with you." "When are you free, are you free at 10:50 or 12:20?" All of that is all part of the training.

'The other thing was that he focuses a lot on making sure that you understand what the client wants – and that's where the famous story about the umbrella being bought for sun, not rain, protection comes in.

'This is the story that Steve often refers to, and, unless you ask the question, how do you know the answer?

Back at Otis UK, we are soon getting used to the idea of asking big questions. '"So how would you like it; would you like it red or black?" The answer to that one is: "I don't really know," because it's a closed question. "How do you want to develop your business? How do you see the landscape in the industry moving forward? Does the current economic scene affect the way that you're developing your strategy?" Those are the open questions: it's the who, what, why questions that you should include in your everyday interactions with customers.

'The famous incident with Steve happens when we're having a conference down in Gien, in France and we're taking all the sales people down to see a new product. We are not really trying to do sales training as such but we want to show them the new product and emphasise the value proposition.

'By this stage he is very much part of the team, he knows everybody. But one of the things I say to Steve is: "I need to warn you about Roy, my boss." "Roy," I tell him, "actually thinks you're a bullshitter and you need to tone it down it a bit. You need to "drop your pants," mate, just calm it all down." So he says: "Oh right, I get your drift."

'So anyway, he stands up and drops his pants. Just like that! 'Now I look back, I have to say it's more funny after the event than at the time because everyone just thinks, what the fuck's that all about?' Years later, Roy and I have a good laugh about it. Roy says: "I can't believe that you can get a man to stand up in front of 50 people and drop his pants." I say: "Well yeah, there you go, that's the power of persuasion."

'There's no two ways about it, success brings success and in the UK in the early nineties, we are really starting to enjoy what we are doing. It's a whole lot of fun. The other great thing about this era, you know, the four or five years we are talking about, is that we never lose a sales person.

'We have no attrition whatsoever. We have extraordinary loyalty and a lot of camaraderie.

'We then build out a very interesting strategy with the sales people at another launch in Sardinia. That is when I lay out our objective of 60, 30, 15, 1. So I put it all up on the screen: here's our objective, 60, 30, 15, 1. They all say: "What's that all about?"

'So the objective is actually very straightforward, every salesman is expected to sell at least 60 lifts per annum. If we sell 60 lifts per annum we will end up with a 30% market share, so we are looking to get 30% market share minimum. Of course, you know market dynamics probably prevent you going too far down that route, but, here's the thing, we actually do much better than that because we are that successful.

'Our objective is 60 for the salesmen, 30% market share, and we put another marker in the sand: we want a 15% margin. Everybody thinks I am off my trolley then, they really think I'm crazy, it's never going to happen!

'The 1 is for the construction team around the hours that we sell for the installation of the lift so they will complete the installation within the hours that we sold. In other words, at a multiple of 1 or 100%, if you understand what I mean.

'When you're selling a lift, you've got material and labour. The labour is all about the hours that you need from them to install the lift. Let's assume you've sold 100 hours. If you have 100 hours allowed and you utilise 100 hours, 100 into 100 is 1.

'If you utilise 105 hours but you only sold 100, you've installed it in a multiple of 1.05. If you sold 100 and you did 95 hours you've done it in a multiple of 0.95. The construction multiple is important when we are doing the pricing strategy because if we are selling at

100 and consistently taking, let's say 10% more, the average for the construction of the part would be 1.1 and we would have to change our pricing strategy – and up our hours.

'So 60, 30, 15, 1 was what we set up and as I say, come '97, when I went off to the States we are at £90 million from £30 million and up to a 15% margin from zero.

'In all of this, Steve is, if you like, behind the scenes. He is the conductor and maybe I am in the wind section, I don't really know or maybe the drum section beating the drum.

'But as a collective of sales managers, myself and Steve, we are able to bring to Otis UK a highly successful thing.

'The good news about that era is that we have the construction team increasingly improving its efficiency so that even when we are growing the sales, we do not have to worry about whether we have the resources or not because they have the volume to learn on.

'The last, but not least, thing was that the value proposition starts to impact our approach to major projects. We take on a dedicated sales manager, in fact we make him a sales director, Joe Kilgallen. He is mighty successful in selling big projects and in '95-'96 we secure £25 million worth of business with one client. This is a major breakthrough with Bovis Stanhope and we truly become the market leader.'

If you want to change habits and processes in a company, start from top to bottom, so the whole company is walking the talk.

• • •

If everyone is working to the same inspiring goals and processes, and enjoying them, it will positively influence your employee loyalty and lower your attrition rate.

• • •

Continuously question the current psychology you work with, even if it's successful and set your ego aside to welcome external feedback.

• • •

Get very clear on your value proposition. Make sure you understand what the client wants and how your product can fulfil this need or desire. Ask big, open questions, then funnel down until you get them to say 'Yes.'

For every bit of value that you give,
make sure you receive a bit of commitment
from the client in return. Make them feel like
they are already 'invested' – even if it's 'just'
time and energy.

• • •

Set inspiring objectives and work your way
back to their origin, so you can get a clear
action plan ready.

• • •

Look at the success rate of each step in the
process and use that to set targets.

• • •

Focus on proactive lead generation; this is the
origin of the final amount of sales.

There Has to Be a No

CHAPTER TEN

I am in Singapore on an important video conference. My body clock is telling me it's some time next week. That's because I left New York 16 hours earlier. In all, I've had a total of 12 hours' sleep in the last 5 days.

'The video conference is being held from the East Coast of the US. It's not that I'm not interested. But I am desperately trying to stay awake, trying to concentrate, trying to participate, trying to add value.

'But, Shit, no! The wave hits: I'm falling asleep over the laptop. It is close to impossible because I've done my day's job, in fact I've done my two days' job. Now I've got to hang around here. And, worse still, my colleagues can see that I am losing it.

How do I first meet Sandy Diehl? Well, the story starts really with Otis Worldwide deciding to centralise the operation in the US. Up until 1997 the company is operating in four zones, Europe, Asia, Americas and indeed Southern Americas.

'Otis, the clear market leader up until that point, starts to see a massive threat coming from KONE with the launch of a machine room-less product called MonoSpace.

'There are accusations flying about that the Otis people in Europe have taken their eye off the ball and allowed KONE to do it. But the European leaders of Otis are saying there's really no need to worry because the machine room-less product has been innovated by Otis in Japan many years earlier.

'Anyway, I think the main reason is that Otis decide they need to get going as a global player rather than an international company: the distinction is obviously having global products not localised ones.

'So, the decision is to globalise the company. We are soon shutting down the zonal offices in Paris and Singapore and San Paulo

Otis Senior VP, Strategy and Development, Sandy Diehl's great insight still rings in my ears: 'There has to be a No.' He did a lot to help me and my family integrate into US life. He was hugely intelligent, but I did manage to teach him one word, 'secondment', which he hadn't heard of before. That proves us Brixton boys do know a thing or two.

as we globalise and this guy Steve Page is appointed as the CEO. He's come from United Technologies, the owner of Otis, and indeed he's been the CFO there before coming onto the CEO role in Otis. 'Steve appoints a completely new team of people, one of them being Sandy Diehl as the Senior Vice President of Product Strategy. 'The interesting thing about that appointment is that, until then, everybody recognises it is about sales and marketing – but here was this new emphasis on product strategy, so much so that the title is changed to announce to the world of Otis that we would have a single person responsible for what products that we were going to make and sell. Sandy gets the brief.

'In turn, Sandy has to have his own team of people and, because the emphasis was on product strategy, he wants to have product managers or product directors responsible for the main product lines of the company.

'In this case we are talking about high-rise products, low-rise products, escalators, service products and modernisation products, with all that under his team whereas marketing communications was a separate organisation.

'So the clear focus of Sandy's team is to contain these product leaders and to define the strategies for the particular product line.

'I'm not too sure at the time if Sandy has an engineering degree but he is extremely well-qualified and ultimately, he holds a Harvard MBA. I also know that he's had a short spell out in one of the locations or districts of Otis North America and he clearly must have been in a prominent role in Otis North America to be identified as the Senior Vice President of Otis Worldwide.

'Sandy is younger, probably five years younger than me, let's say he is, you know, a contrast to some of the other people that we've spoken about who walk through the door.

'He certainly isn't a guy who is smartly dressed or anything like that but there is one thing about him: he seems to glow with a warmth about him and I suppose because of his position as well, he is a person of real influence. When you speak to him you know that you are talking with a top-level guy. He's not assertive, but persuasive, and has an incredible capability of asking big questions and making you think. He also allows people space to excel in their roles. He's from New Jersey, I believe, a family man and a good, good guy.

'Now Sandy, he's got to go and find the product leaders and I'm not too sure of the process he actually uses because he inherits some of the people from the demise of the regional organisation.

'The guy that is heading up the low-rise business is a guy called Fernando Rico. He's based in Paris, a Spanish guy, incredibly knowledgeable, and a fantastic engineer. Then there is Ron Beaver in charge of high-rise products, who's an American and who knows the high-rise factory set up well. Then there is the escalator guy, who more or less has to come from within the escalator factory environment in Germany, so Michael Fohrer gets the role for escalators. The service guy is an Italian guy, Sergio de Luca, so that leaves just one spot open; for modernisation.

'So we, in the operations, in the various countries, we are interested to see how this is all going to manifest itself and who is going to do what. All this coincides with a situation involving Roy Markham, who is still working at Otis at the time where he is now the Managing Director of the Express Evans Lift Company.

'Very sadly there has been a fatality in the UK.

'Under the then rules of United Technology, the principal of a company where there's been a fatality has to attend the United Technologies Board Meeting and explain exactly how and why it has happened. And, at UTC, you could never question their commitment to safety.

'George David is the CEO of UTC at this time and so Roy Markham has to go to Connecticut to present to the UTC Board all the events and circumstances leading up to the fatality. It's pretty common knowledge that anyone who gets themselves into that situation is probably going to get just one answer out of the Board, the Lord Sugar one: "You're fired."

'Roy does everything possible to explain the situation, he has a working model made and tries to go through how this guy has contravened the working regulations. Then he comes up with the most notorious quote of the whole episode, and that is: "You can take a horse to water but you can't make it drink." "Unfortunately, with all this training and all the rest of it, the guy still didn't follow the rules," says Roy, or words to that effect. George David apparently turns round to Roy and says: "It's your job to make them drink." So, Roy gets fired.

'While all this was taking place, Steve Page and his new entourage of Sandy Diehl and a few of the other new Senior Vice Presidents are doing a tour round the world to see what they had actually got hold of now that they had taken charge.

'They all come to the UK and one of the main places to see is the Otis Liverpool factory. We are preparing for the "royal" factory visit and the Otis UK Managing Director, Jack Leingang, calls me up the night before the visit to the factory and says: "I won't be coming to the factory visit with Steve Page."

'I say: "You're kidding me aren't you, you've got to be there." He says: "No, no something more serious has cropped up." So I say: "Well whatever it is it must be really serious." He says: "I can tell you it's serious." Well, it transpires he is having to deal with the sudden dismissal of Roy Markham and he can't be in two places at once, so I am nominated as the main Otis UK person to meet the entourage.

'So, for the first time, I meet all these top people. To be totally honest with you, while I treat them with the utmost respect, of course, they don't actually mean too much to me. I am not overawed by their presence. I've met George David, the main man of United Technologies, on three previous occasions so it all falls into a certain level of perspective.

'Nonetheless, I take on the responsibility of showing them around the factory and my main goal is to present to them the need for the Liverpool factory to be part of the new regime, because the skillset and the quality of the production from the factory in Liverpool is world class. It is essential, certainly from our point of view, to keep the factory thriving. We think that it has to be part of the future consideration for the product offering. So I give a pretty passionate presentation.

'Steve Page is an incredibly easy guy to get on with, Sandy Diehl is this warm guy who's got immediate empathy with me – it just turns out that he's a Virgo and I'm a Virgo and apparently Virgos get on well with each other.

'Anyway, we're walking around the factory and chatting and then Sandy says to me: "You know all about my new structure." So I reply: "Yeah, it seems a pretty good idea." But I didn't think over the matter too much and then he says: "I'm looking for somebody to lead the modernisation business." So I say: "Oh really, well, that's a challenge and a half, that's not an easy role." So he says: "No, no, I've got a few people that I'm considering." He floats some names to me and, in my naivete, I say: "Well these people aren't influential enough in the world of Otis. You need somebody that's got a track record that people will listen to." So he says: "Yeah and it's what I'm really worried about: who is the right person?"

'So off they go, they all leave Liverpool and I make my way back to London a couple of days later, meet up with Jack, and we review what's gone on. He tells me all about the unfortunate situation of Roy Markham. Jack was pretty upset about that, but that's life in the corporate world.

'Jack says to me: "Bill, you're now my righthand man in this company." So I am very pleased to hear this. Then, a couple of weeks later, he pipes up: "How did the interview go?" Jack, so dry with his humour. I say to him: "What interview?" He says: "The interview with Sandy Diehl." So I say: "I haven't had an interview with Sandy Diehl, where's this coming from?" He says: "Well you may not have known that you were in an interview but you were in an interview." So I say: "Really?" So I say: "When was that? I honestly thought I was losing, you know!" He says: "No when you were walking round the factory they were very, very impressed with you and they want to offer you a job." So I say: "You're kidding me, aren't you?" So he says: "No, I think it'd be a great move." So I say: "Oh right." He says: "You've got to go over there for what is almost an endorsement to the selection... you're not being interviewed."

'So off I go, fly over to the US, meet up with Sandy Diehl, he tells me all about how he sees the role, why they think I'm the best person to do the job. Then I do a tour of all the other senior vice presidents who are working for Steve Page: the engineering guy, Ray Mancini, and I have to meet up with the logistics factory guy, the French guy, I can't remember his name, and then I have to meet up with the senior vice president of human resources, Paul Thomson.

'So I do the full round robin and, later in the evening I am invited to attend a dinner at a fantastic restaurant not too far from Hartford, on the river there. It is for one of the senior engineers of Otis Worldwide who's retiring. It is my first experience of being in amongst an American-type event and they do a roasting of this guy and I'm sitting there and I just couldn't believe what they are saying. I mean they rip this guy apart and the whole place is in hilarious uproar. I don't know anything that was going on, I just think the whole situation is pretty comical, let alone what was being said. Anyway, so it's all obviously done in incredibly good humour and a great evening. 'Then it comes to Steve Page standing up and saying to this guy, congratulations on your 40 years' service, and your well-deserved retirement. In his speech to this guy he turns 'round and looks me straight in the face and he says, "Bill, we have a great time over here, we're looking forward to you joining us."

'I think: I didn't know I had the job until that evening! I think: Oh My God, what's this all about? It is so different. So the following day I'm meeting up with Paul Thomson and I am just on a rollercoaster: "So, Paul, Steve Page says I got the job." "Oh yeah, yeah that's Steve's way. All we've got to do is work out when you're starting." I say: "Well no-one's told me how much I'm going to get paid. What is the deal?"

'He says: "Don't worry, that will all be sorted out in due course." 'So here I am, I go back to Jack Leingang in the UK and I say: "Jack they've offered me the job as the Product Director for Modernisation, it's a great opportunity and I'd like to take the job because it's

The Evans family circa. 1997. Here we are up the Empire State Building on our orientation visit to the USA. The gorilla obviously got to George, who, much to my regret, did not move to the US. Our five years in the US was an amazing experience which provides endless stories for Sue to tell. Emily ended up marrying Nick from New York State. We now have two US grandkids, Rhys and Isla.

a career step forward." So he says: "It's well justified, you know the business inside out." For a lot of my career up until then I'd been involved in modernisation so I am not walking into a job that I don't know anything about, I know it well.

'So, anyway, there I am, the next step is to get the family to go over to the US on a reconnaissance trip and we go around the schools and we set up various house viewings and stuff like that.

'The one unfortunate thing about it all is that my son is in the final year of college in the UK so it just doesn't make any sense for him to come with us too. Probably, from a family or personal family point of view that decision is a big mistake. We should have insisted, but he doesn't come over.

'Meanwhile, thanks to Sandy Diehl, Emily, who's the younger one and just 15, gets into a fantastic school, Kingswood Oxford which is in Hartford. It's a top of the range school which Otis pays for, giving her a great education. She goes on to university in Boston, does a degree in psychology and onto a Masters degree down in New York. Today she's got a fantastic job. We are always grateful to Sandy for creating that opportunity for her. She ends up marrying an American guy and they've got two kids so we've now got American grandkids. But that's all down to Sandy from the get-go.

'So we're right into the job and it is an interesting thing because there is a bit of an embargo on travel at the time I join Otis in the States, which is quite amusing really because without travel you can't even begin to do the job. Bearing in mind we're talking 24 years ago, video conferencing and the like was not as it is today.

'So you have to make your way around the full territory and unless you know your markets you can't really perform. Anyway, while there is a bit of an embargo on, one of the things they do set up in my induction is for me to go to the Ito University. That's a university for quality set up by UTC and named after Yuzuru Ito. The sessions are held in the US, at Hartford, and I'm only part of all the United Technology participants, plus I'm the only guy from oversees, due to this travel ban, and I'm also the only person from Otis too.

'I'm in amongst a lot of aircraft engineers, Pratt & Whitney, Hamilton, Sikorski, I believe there were some people there from Carrier, from UTC fuel sales, so there's a whole myriad of people but they were predominantly airplane engineers.

'I learnt a helluva lot about the quality tools, Six Sigma, and so on, but there's always one thing that sticks in my mind. It makes me laugh because it epitomises how you should understand what quality really means to you as an individual.

'One day we have a session and we're talking about "turnbacks."

'Now in my world that's a breakdown, or in the world of lifts these are often known as call-outs, but in their aeronautical world they call them turnbacks. They are busy talking about turnbacks, or breakdown rates, and there's this persistent talk about "IFSD." So they kept on talking about IFSDs and there I am sitting there thinking, do you know what, I haven't got a clue what they're talking about. I feel a little bit intimidated because all these Americans are big, hunky, Chuck type guys with deep voices: "God Dammit, the IFSDs" and so on.

'In the end I think: This is stupid. They're talking about this for about 15 minutes and so I very timidly put my hand up and I say: "Excuse me, I don't know what you're talking about."

'You can imagine it, it's like a tennis match, all of a sudden all the heads turn and they're all looking at me. This guy says: "You don't know what IFSDs are?" Accusing me! I say: "No I haven't got a clue." "In flight shut-downs." So I say: "In flight shut-down." He says: "Yes." I say: "You've just been talking about IFSDs and the rate on this particular Pratt & Whitney engine is 45%." He says: "Yeah." I say: "That can't be right." So there was a chuckle in the room and we're all having a bit of a laugh about it and they say: "Yeah it is right."

'So I say: "Hold on a second, let me get this right. You are saying that these engines on a United Airline have got a shut-down rate of 45%." "Yes, in flight shut down." So I say: "Well no wonder you're losing market share to Rolls Royce." He says: "Oh yeah, but we've got four engines." Well in those days they have four engines on the bloody planes, so no wonder they can get these 45% shut-down rates.

'What is going through my mind is: here I am on the quality university and I'm thinking what is quality all about.

'I was using this during a lecture only the other day, if you go on your holiday and you go up the steps into the plane, whether it's easyJet or British Airways, doesn't matter, and on the side of the door it says we're really proud to announce that the In Flight Shut Down rate on this plane is 45%, would you go on holiday? The answer is: No. Would you go on holiday if it says 90%? The answer is: no you wouldn't. You'd get on that plane with all the confidence in the world that the engine is not going to fail. So that's quality. Quality is all about expecting it to work, expecting it not to break down, expecting it to do what you want it to do. Here we are with a bunch of American guys in engineering manufacturing accepting the quality can be less than 100%. I am astounded!

'So I've now got this in my head, quality, quality, quality. I am lucky later on in the career, working with Sandy, to go to Japan and start to realise that quality has a serious meaning for the Japanese – and no wonder I'm on a Japanese-inspired quality university because you've just got to change your mindset.

'So, I've now finished my induction, been 'round various people, been to the university and I'm now getting stuck into the job. I've got to formulate the strategy for the modernisation business and I lean on the tool that I was given many years ago by Ken Myers which is an established tool of the marketing mix, the four Ps.

'I just think that quality is what I've got to develop and I then start to present and get feedback on whether people buy into it.

'I know there is an emphasis on the product and, in modernisation or refurbishment, the products could be sub-component type products; it doesn't have to be a holistic lift system in itself. I work a lot on all of that sort of stuff and there I am in consultation with Sandy and the other groups, and I shared my presentation with them all, and I have some great people working alongside me.

'Also, I have the good fortune of having Robin Fiala working with me on the modernisation business, a very educated lady, with lots of pragmatic experience working as a location manager originally down in Manhattan at the Rockefeller Center. We work on all that.

'Anyway we're debating each of our strategies because, as a complete unit, product strategy, we all have to have our speech. And one of the most profound things that Sandy comes out with to all of us is: "Where's the "No?" To be honest with you I don't quite grasp what he is saying. He says that for any strategy, it doesn't matter how complex it is, you have to have boundaries. You can't do everything, you can't be all things to all men, you must have a "No" and your "No" has to be cast-iron otherwise you're going to be shooting moose all over the place and you can only shoot the moose where the moose are.

'Here's a man who's a Harvard MBA, all the rest of it, but able to communicate a simple thing that is so powerful and so profound. I've taken it from there onwards, we can't do everything, we've got to have a "No." Even the people in D2E repeat back to me "No," we've got to have a "No." So, we live that.

'Anyway, during the time working with Sandy we are now faced with the challenge of coming up with a complete competitive response to KONE MonoSpace. That is the main objective of the group – even though we have all our individual product responsibilities – collectively we have to work on coming up with a product response.

'There are various scenarios discussed, but, fortunately, one of Otis' smart engineers comes up with the use of the flat belt which is most commonly found as the cam belt in a car. That brilliant flat belt idea gives us the opportunity to use a much smaller diameter driving sheave on the motor which means it could use a much smaller motor – and a smaller motor could go at the top of the lift shaft.

'The Gen 2 product is born.

'It is around this time that we are all focusing on what we are doing but as I say the biggest conversation was around Gen 2. We're doing really well, there's Steve Page who has shut down all the regional engineering projects and we have to focus on the ones we're not going to do. So the "No" strategy came into play big time then. "Right," we would say, "Let's look at this list" – it was a monumental list of engineering projects – which ones are we not going to do anymore? We won't fund this and we're going to focus.

'So now we're probably six to nine months away from the big launch of Gen 2 and I happen to be with Sue and the kids, we have been away for a long weekend in Barbados.

'There's no mobile phones, virtually nothing, come to think of it, we may have had one of the first mobile phones about this time. Anyway, just before I'm coming back to the US, it's only a short distance away, Barbados, I don't know if I've got a message or if I phone into the office but anyway I speak to our PA, Sharon: "Any messages, everything okay?" She says: "Yes, Bill, we want you, you've got to come into the office early on the Monday because we've got a worldwide video conference and it's at 5am in the morning." Well, 5am in the morning is quite normal because we have to work around the time zones, but she says: "No you need to come in before 5am, Sandy wants to see you."

'So I go in about 4.30am, he's there going to his office. I say: "Hi Sandy, you want to see me?" He says: "Yes." He puts his hand out to shake my hand which in a way is unusual. The French do it all the time, but the Americans don't do it unnecessarily.

'He puts his hand out and says: "Congratulations." So I say: "Congratulations for what?" He says: "You are now Vice President." So needless to say I am taken back, I say: "What's that about? It's obviously fantastic recognition." So he says: "No, you're the best person really to help drive through the launch of Gen 2, you need to work with Fernando on that, you've got Robin now who can focus more on the modernisation so we want you to be the VP of Product Management rather than product strategy."

'The title is to put more emphasis on the globalised basis of the role because Fernando isn't based in the US and I think that there is a need to have more of an international flavour to product strategy. I think I've also got recognition as an individual, as someone that is influential, but I don't know.

'The amusing thing here is that now, at 4.30am, I'm suddenly a Vice President and at 5am Sandy announces to the world that I'm Vice President of Product Management.

'Once again, I haven't got a clue if I'm going to get more money or less money or whatever. You just get on with it, which I am happy to do, more than happy to do. It is wonderful. When I think right back to the days with Jimmy Giles, walking around Dolphin Square, and here I am now as Vice President with the privilege of parking my car in the front parking lot at WHQ – and part of the United Technologies structure in terms of grading and all that – it is incredible to me... but like everything else, it turns out it's not quite as smooth as you might want it to be.

'The biggest problem of all is that there is a rule within United Technologies that anybody going into this grading, ie the level that I am being introduced to, following George David's requirement, has to have an MBA. Well, I have an MBA in life, my university was Brixton, and walking the streets of Brixton and going to the Ram Jam Club and all of that, but I don't have an MBA from Harvard at this stage.

'The twist to it all is that here I am being told you haven't got an MBA, you've got the job, but you've still got to do an MBA. The human resource department sits me down and selects a university for me to go off and do an MBA at. At the same time I'm taking on this much bigger role which necessitates me travelling even more around the world. It is quite a bizarre combination, but anyway I start the programme with the Heriot-Watt University in Edinburgh.

'Apart from all the other things I'm doing, I'm also the chairman of the Otis university for sales and marketing. I always remember Robin coming into my office and saying: "Do you know this is a joke. You've got to do an MBA and yet you do lectures on price management." I say: "Well yeah but rules are rules, you've got to follow through on them."

'So, working with Sandy has some fantastic excitements, we

launch Gen 2, we then start working on what is known as the Next Step Escalator which was the most revolutionary escalator design from any manufacturer.

'Unfortunately, it never ends up in full production, and there are some political reasons for that, but it is all about the supply chain not actually being properly scrutinised in China (through no fault of the Chinese) – it's just that it isn't scrutinised adequately. The fundamental improvement with the Next Step Elevator is that there is no main chain, and each step is a cog with the skirt panel integrated with the step. In other words, there is never any danger of anyone getting their foot sucked in the side of the escalator because the side is all part of the step. So, with an escalator, people see the steps and, at the top and bottom, they see the flat steps but then there's also the threshold of the escalator which is where the motor and the engine are located.

'Thanks to this new technology, that piece of the escalator uses a lot less space. So if you're a developer with a need to have an opening in, say, an atrium, which is 30m wide accommodating the escalator, you could actually opt for a narrower atrium because your escalator's not going to take up so much space. There are some really big advantages with the product but it is totally reliant on absolute precision in the dimensions of each sub component. If there was ever any excessive tolerance you would end up with the thing piling up and unfortunately inferior quality metal is used.

'So that project fails – for lack of proper quality control – but it is an exciting time running up to that. We do other exciting things and travel round the world. We are involved in projects in Japan and Singapore and Australia, even down in Brazil, and all the time we are working with Sandy in the Worldwide quarters: it is an exciting time.

'There are occasions where people would say: "I don't know how you manage to do all the travelling, how are you getting on with jet lag?" I would say: "It's very simple, I just have jet lag all the time so I don't know life without jet lag." But, sure enough, it starts to take its toll.

The map is not the territory. Coloured in orange are the countries I visited during my five years working at Otis World Headquarters in Connecticut USA. More than two million air miles, accompanied by numerous bouts of jet lag. The experience stood me in good stead to start D2E International.

'When you're working in that type of corporate role, the roller-coaster is out of control and you've got to watch out. Corporations should be looking at individuals doing these types of roles like that and say, from a wellbeing point of view, is this right? 'Back to that terrible video conference in Singapore. The conference is being held from the US, so there I am at 1am trying to stay awake, trying to concentrate, trying to participate, trying to add value and I'm falling asleep over the laptop and it is close to impossible because you've done way more than your day's job, you've got to hang around and there you are, nodding off.

'Then Lo and Behold! in the middle of the night the phone rings and it's Sharon from the States saying: "Bill, wake up, your daughter's totalled the car." At the time I don't know what "totalled" means so I say: "What, what are you talking about she's totalled the car?" "She's had a car accident, she's totalled it."

'Well, it's an Americanism, not an Englishism, it transpires that my daughter has been driving to school in her Beetle one morning, going down the hill towards Kingswood, Oxford. She's clipped the kerb or something or other and this brand new Volkswagen Beetle literally has turned over and rolled over several times and, in my language, it is a complete write-off.

'Fortunately, all the airbags have come out and her life has been spared, she is okay, her worst bruising has been mental, but the car is a wreck, or in other American words: "totalled." But here I am, over in Singapore, helpless. My wife Susan's saying: "Oh My God this job is too much, you're over in Singapore, when are you getting back?"

'I'm not scheduled to be back for three days, I try to change my flights, it's not easy when you're over there, I am able to get back one day earlier but that's no good because two and a half days have gone by. All of those things, the glory of the job... actually there's no glory in those jobs at all. It's full-on pressure. I won't say it's stress, but it's definitely pressure.

'My five years working with Sandy is incredibly educational, I'm forever grateful to him for career progression, what I learn from him and what he does for my family. But on the other side of the coin, there is the unrelenting pressure of the job, the splitting up of the family, leaving my son behind, even if Emily thrives because of her education, with my wife, Sue, spending many a week, not just a day, many a week, without me because I am always travelling. It's no wonder that people go on to have breakdowns.

'Now, because of, I suppose, my resilience brought about by my upbringing and some of the Jimmy Giles stuff that was early formed, I am able to cope with it all but I have to say my health suffers in the end.

'My blood pressure is eventually running at a level that forces me to take time off work to calm down and then I suppose this is when the famous "No" comes right back into play. I'm not doing this job anymore.

'I am fortunate enough to be able to take early retirement because Otis is now restructuring, with political manoeuvres worthy of a Spielberg blockbuster. Dallas' JR would learn some technique from this story! That's for another day.

'All I would say is that I learn a huge amount working in that role. The fundamental of the "No" is great, the attitude to quality changed me dramatically and my international awareness is second to none now.

'The enjoyment of working on the Otis University and along-side some incredibly talented people and helping them reach their potential has been one of the most enriching things I have ever done. I can put the lifestyle of being a VP in America like this: you have to pinch your bum to say, is this really happening to us? It is incredible. Thanks to Sandy, I would say yes to it all over again, but he also taught me a vital corporate safeword.

'He taught me how to say "No."'

It's important to focus on quality, and to think about what quality means to you.
Learn to say 'No' to whatever doesn't measure up to your quality standards.

• • •

For every strategy, you need boundaries. You can't be everything to everyone. Learn to say 'No' to clients, projects and approaches that don't fit your vision.

• • •

Even if you are resilient, not listening to your body takes its toll in the end. Learn to say 'No' to opportunities, tasks and travel assignments when your body needs more rest and balance (or your body will say no for you, in the end).

• • •

Companies should keep an eye on the wellbeing of individuals that are taking a lot on their plate.

Even if the job seems glorious, pay attention to
what you are giving up for that 'glory.'
In the end it might not be worth missing out on
precious time with your family.

• • •

Learn how to say 'No' to opportunities that
have a negative impact on your personal
relationships and family life.

• • •

It's very useful to grow international awareness.
Unless you really know your markets, it's hard
to perform.

They are Telling You Something

CHAPTER ELEVEN

Towards the end of the 1990s an important meeting occurs. One by one, the operating divisions of United Technology Corporation are taking its chief executive through their units' financial results.

One managing director has more reason than the rest to be confident in his division's performance; all his numbers are looking strong. As he finishes with a flourish the chief executive interrupts him: "May we take a look at your employee satisfaction?"

The managing director is taken aback and hesitant to get into details, but the chief executive insists. He knows full well that the managing director's staff morale score is one of the lowest in all of UTC's divisions.

Finally, the chief executive addresses the crestfallen director: "Your employees are telling you what your next financial results will be."

'Let's talk about George David: I mean this is a man!
'Funnily enough I have very little direct experience of him actually being in a meeting. The only time I've met George is when he's wanted me for a particular reason.

'When I work over in America, for instance, I host a confidential tour of the Otis Test Tower. George has some very important potential Far East guests he is trying to coax into UTC.

'He wants to showcase the world of Otis and, because of my position in the company, I am the one nominated to host George and these people around the facilities.

'I am not somebody he doesn't know, but, as I say, I give the tour, all the presentations in a walk-and-talk when he wants to show these people something.

George David, former chairman and chief executive officer of United Technologies Corporation, was a man I first met back in 1983 when Otis launched REM 2. I was fortunate enough to meet George several times subsequently in my career. The last occasion was when I helped host a VIP visit to the Otis Test Tower in Connecticut, when I had the balls to correct George on a particular subject. Weeks later, he signed off my promotion.

'A bit bashfully I say to George: "I don't think that's a good move purely because your future partners actually have something better than the thing you want to show them."

'He doesn't take it that well, but, to my relief, he does take it on board.

'George David is highly intelligent. One of his greatest personal attributes is that he can speed-read a book in a couple of hours, he has just an amazing memory.

'He joins Otis, I don't know when, then, from being a regional director he becomes the CEO of Otis and in fact that's when I first meet him, when he is CEO of Otis and, you know, we've spoken about the Brighton experience when he asks me to trial REM 2 and so on.

'So, I meet him on quite a few occasions. He does an amazing job at Otis and from there he becomes the CEO of United Technologies and definitely provides shareholder value. He is focused!

'He has centralised all United Technologies. We all go to Farmington, Carrier comes in and then subsequently they buy Chubb. He's been instrumental in quite a few of the bigger acquisitions.

'There's actually a rivalry between UTC and General Electric. That seems to be the Jack Welsh vs George David story. So there's lots of stuff been written about George.

'The second occasion I meet George David – years earlier – is when I become the marketing manager and part of my responsibilities involves company-wide communications.

'The company newspaper has been renamed Going Up by a guy that came into Otis for a short time, Brian King, so we always used to joke: "What did Brian King ever do?" Well, he renamed the magazine Going Up, but Brian King is an amazing guy for all sorts of other reasons too.

'Anyway, George does his tour of the Otis companies and he comes to Otis UK and it is quite something to watch him go to work on tour. What I like about the guy is that he really is at the top of his game but he is also very appreciative of, and gives full recognition to, the field workers.

'He is able to work on different levels and I remember there is this breakfast meeting that we have to organise – I mean we have all these breakfast meetings for George to go to – and it is all very well-orchestrated in advance.

'For instance, he wants to know: "What do the guys have for breakfast?" Someone sort of says: "Well, they all have bacon rolls." So he says: "Right, so we'll have bacon roll breakfast meetings for the Otis UK team." Knowing George, I suppose they'll have croissant meetings for the French guys, I don't really know, but I suspect they would do. Anyway, we have these meetings and George is the only one allowed to speak, none of the Otis UK managers can speak; he is talking direct to the people and trying to engage with the field guys.

'Something comes up about some development on an Otis job and George turns round to me and he says: "How come these guys don't know anything about this project?" I don't recall the specifics. But I do say: "It's in the company magazine, that's how we…" So right off the bat this field guy pipes up: "We don't get a copy of that." 'George turns to me again and he says: "Why aren't these guys getting a copy of the thing?" I say: "We send them out through the field managers." He said: "Why aren't they sent to the home?"

'I say: "We don't have the budget for that." He looks at me and said: "Are you kidding me?" I think: "Holy Shit, I think I've put my foot in this one." So I quickly reply: "But they will be sent out from now on."

'Well you can imagine what a quick swoop of a decision that we have! I forget now how many people we have working for Otis UK in those days but it is one hell of a lot of people: 1,500 maybe, something like that. Imagine that we're now sending out the company magazine, four times a year, direct to their homes. You start to add the cost up….but George is determined.

'Afterwards he says: "You know, communication to the field people: it's absolutely essential."

'Then he actually starts to instigate employee satisfaction surveys right across all the Otis companies. This seems a bit of a strange one really because no-one has even really thought about these things before.

'We're in the late '8os, let's say '88-'89. The survey is being done externally by an agency. I think the whole purpose behind these surveys is that if the employees aren't smiling they can't be smiling at the customer; that's my take on it at least.

'Even when you look at a great customer satisfaction result, that can be because an employee has gone that extra mile – so they really must be happy in their job. Contrast that with the famous Video Arts film by John Cleese many years ago, *Who sold you this then?* which shows that the employee can absolutely crucify a company with the comments that they make to the client.

'So employees are incredibly important but, as a business leader, you have to start to question the information: are you being given what you want to hear or are they giving you what you should hear? 'There's a subtlety in terms of how you can get to that because, you're going to always get some people who are subservient to the boss and they won't actually tell you what you need to hear, they'll tell you what they think you should hear.

'Back to George David: he is so dedicated to employee satisfaction that when he becomes United Technologies chief, he looks at the employee satisfaction scoreboard by all the operating companies at board level.

'That's when the famous story took place about him and the managing director of one of the operating units.

'I thought that his observation to the MD was so astute. If the employees are dissatisfied how the hell can you expect to have good business results? You may be able to ride the market for a while but ultimately customer satisfaction will plummet. So employee satisfaction is a precursor to your results. There're loads of things that you can be measuring around staff such as the attrition rate, people leaving and doing exit interviews, and all the smart things surrounding them.

'But one of the things that I find the most powerful of all is to do your own survey, and conduct it personally.

'I call this "Pulse", you know, as in feeling the pulse. I think that some other organisations do similar sorts of things but the Pulse Meeting to me is meeting somebody on their own ground, not on your ground. So, if a café for the field workers is a comfortable zone for them, their own comfort zone, then that's where you should meet them.

'The other thing is that the Pulse Meeting shouldn't be mechanistic in terms of: 'Well, I'm giving you half an hour to talk to me because I'm a busy man and I've got to go.' That, to me, is not setting the scene for getting feedback on what they really think about the company.

'So the pulse meeting has to be as comfortable, and I'm using that word deliberately, as comfortable as possible for the person that you're talking to, rather than interviewing. You've got to allow people to open up and I find that kind of a meeting extremely beneficial.

'Of course, you do have all these wonderful tools that people have developed, you know, the employee engagement rating and all these different formulae for employee satisfaction. To a large degree they do work but, as I say, my preference is for talking in person, making sure that they feel comfortable talking to you and give you proper feedback on where the company is at.

'You can only probably do that if you've got a small enough enterprise and there's no way could you do it for 50,000 people or something like that. Nevertheless, if you do have a very large workforce the most important thing is to have proper sampling per work group – whether it's the factory guys or the field guys, or the salesforce or the local management, or whatever. The most important thing is to dive into a really good sample.

'The interesting thing in the last couple of years since Covid and the lockdown is the huge amount of change around homeworking, flexi-working and all the rest of it – and how people are actually motivated.

'Employee satisfaction pre-Covid might have been all about the number of initiatives the company's been taking. Then, all of a sudden, people are forced to work from home. Now that they've got the option to work from home the dynamic has completely shifted. Now we will have to see how satisfied our employees are for a new world.

'I truly believe it's even more important to understand employee satisfaction because mental health issues are cropping up quite frequently and a lot of those stem from people not interacting with other human beings.

'Specialists are, of course, being trained to be good mental health counsellors, mentors and all the rest of it, but, in my opinion, you have to look at the root cause of the issue rather than waiting until someone's actually starting to suffer with mental health and then putting a sticking plaster on it. What we need to tackle is the root cause.

'My view is that the root cause of a lot of the issues today is that people aren't in their natural zone and the natural zone is when they're with other people. We are a bird-like species …gregarious.'

'Companies today have to look at how they put even more effort into teamwork and team fun to keep employees satisfied.

'That's not about going over the top and saying party, party, party every day, but about employee satisfaction. Employee satisfaction is a fundamental. We all know the cliché Q: "What's your biggest asset?" A: "Our biggest asset is our employees." Well this is a bit of a corporate spin. On one hand it's a load of bullshit, on the other hand it is bloody obvious.

'Your employees are clearly your biggest asset. It could be argued your biggest asset is your client list but without your employees you aren't going to have any clients – and without clients you won't employ employees. It's circular.

'These days you've got to be fair and, moreover, understand if you're being fair or not being fair. That's why when George says: "Look at your employee satisfaction survey because they're telling you something about where your business is going," it's something that I truly have taken on board in D2E.

'Employee satisfaction is, by the way, not the only thing that

George David gives me. He is a massive advocate of continuous learning.

'It is his belief that everybody has to keep pace with what is going on in the world. So the Darden School of Business (at the University of Virginia) program was something that he pushes out to all the senior levels at UTC to keep them up to speed with the latest thinking.

'Not only does he sponsor my business education at Darden, he comes down and speaks to the delegates that I was with.

'He encourages everybody to get further education and formal qualifications such as an MBA. While the company pays for the course, he also rewards business graduates with stock options as a "well done," you know, recognition.

'I take that same idea when I start D2E. Our vision statement at D2E is to be the most knowledgeable in our field. We back that up with supporting people with continuous learning and rewards in their salary for achieving formal degrees and stuff like that. That's all come from George.

'What about the advice from me that he isn't happy about? Subsequently he feeds back to the CEO of Otis, Steve Page, and says: "Thank Bill for hosting our partners and thank him too for his advice." It is shortly after that that I get my promotion before having an MBA so I guess the advice is not that bad."

Your employee satisfaction is a precursor to
your financial – and other – results.
*If they aren't smiling, they can't smile at
the customers.*
*If they are happy, they are more willing to go
the extra mile for the customer.*
*If they are happy, they aren't complaining or
knocking the company.*

• • •

Check if your employees really are happy.
If using a survey, do this in a subtle way that
allows them to be honest instead of saying what
they think you want to hear.

• • •

Hold your individual feedback and review
meetings on their home turf – so they feel
comfortable in talking to you frankly.

• • •

Keep your employees happy, healthy
and motivated.

Make sure all employees, the field
workers away from head office, are
well-informed about the company's
objectives and bigger picture.

• • •

Give them full recognition.

• • •

Give them real opportunities for learning
and education. Take a deep interest in their
wellbeing and address the root causes of any
mental health issues.
Invest in teamwork and team fun. It's vital
for wellbeing.

• • •

Be honest if you have a well meant, critical
remark on an approach, even if initially it
doesn't land well. They might thank you later.

You Have Never Arrived

It is 2003, just after the start of the new millennium. With a New Labour government headed by a youthful Tony Blair, it is a time of hope and looking forward. Change is afoot.

Bill finds himself amid the birth pangs of a new company. 'We've been building up, if you like, all the commercial collateral, all our value propositions and all the rest of it and then we discover we need to have our own elevator pitch!

'One of the things we do know is sending out emails and stuff like that is just a waste of time.

'So it's a case of picking up the phone and pitching. And the pitch goes like this: "We're an international firm of lift consultants, we've established ourselves now in Europe and, in particular, the UK. If there are any projects that you may want to consider for our unique way of working, we're available." Dah de-dah, de-dah, de-dah.

'Anyway I've got this little annexe to my house. It's like an office set up but without files because we have no files to file!'So I am sitting there and all of a sudden the bloody phone rings. "Oh, Oh My God!" I go, because we have a separate phone line in the annexe and we are using that one as the company phone line. "The phone is ringing!"

"Hello?" "Hello. Is that D2E?" "Yeah, sorry, yeah it's D2E, sorry." 'I am embarrassed about the fact that I haven't even answered the phone properly. "Well this is Robert Cook from Cushman & Wakefield." So I say: "Oh hello Robert, how are you?" "I'm fine," he says, "I've been given your name and company as you do lift consultancy. Do you do surveys, lift surveys?"

"Yeah," I put in quickly. "We do lift surveys." So he says: "We need a survey to be done urgently in a building just off Hanover Square." So I say: "Yeah fine." He says: "It's pretty urgent, when can you get there?"

'So this is the situation: we've got no work and we could go out there immediately. But you don't dare say that because that just shows you've got no work on. So I say to Robert (who is a customer to this day): "Oh Robert, do you mind just giving me a minute, I just need to check my calendar and also my engineer's availability." 'So I'm doing this rustling-of-my papers caper.

'So I come back. "Robert, sorry to keep you waiting, our engineer is in the West End in two days' time around, 11 o'clock, is that soon enough?" "Oh," he says, "that's fantastic." So I say: "Okay, can you send me the details and all the rest of it?"

'So he says: "Yeah, yeah, yeah." He says: "I need to send you a purchase order." So I've said: "Oh yes."

'I'm thinking, Shit! I haven't even thought about a purchase order! So he says: "By the way, how much will the survey be?" I don't have a clue, I really don't know how much to charge. We've done everything to set up the business but the one thing we haven't got to is our pricing structure or our pricing strategy.

'So I say: "Look, if it's a one-off lift, and it's in the West End, it's going to be £600." He says: "Really?" I'm thinking, Shit! I've gone and done it now – it's too much for him. So I say: "Yeah, No, it's £600." So he says: "Oh, you've got very good rates." I think, Shit! I'm too cheap. Two days later I go with Alan Seaton who is working, a school friend of mine, and we'd been working together forever.

'So I say: "Alan we've got to do a survey."

'Up we go onto the site. We have no idea how to do a survey from a consultancy point of view. I mean we obviously know exactly how to look all over the lift and report this and that – but not as consultants.

'So, there I am in the lift pit shining a torch and looking at all the crap in the lift pit and I start laughing to Alan: "Can you believe this?" He says: "What's up, Bill?" I say: "Listen, yesterday I was a bloody vice president of Otis worldwide, today I'm in a lift pit starting a business."

'He says: "Well, you always start the business from the ground upwards, Mate!"

'I eventually leave Otis in 2002 with an 18-month worldwide compromise agreement which means that I mustn't go near anybody in the lift industry that would compromise my release from Otis.

'That gives me a certain amount of time to decide what I want to do and it isn't too long after I stopped working – on 28th February 2002 – that I start to realise that I need to work, not for a financial reason, but more for a mental one because I am just crawling up the wall.

'It isn't a good time, although from a social point of view Sue and I go looking around to buy a holiday home. We are thinking about maybe buying an apartment in Spain or France and so we tour around a fair bit.

'Soon I am starting to get really frustrated and I think, right, I've got to do something.'I am having this idea of offering myself out as a non-exec director and I am a bit naïve about it all at the time but the truth is I am pretty much in a turmoil and I think suddenly, do you know what, why am I fighting with myself as to what I want to do? I know the lift industry and more importantly I love the lift industry, so maybe I better think about something in that.'Well, months slip by and I get a first approach through Roy Markham. I am offered a position with Schindler, based in Switzerland, working on a worldwide basis, in a front-of-house, or customer-role, which sounds pretty appealing. Having said that, it's against the compromise agreement so I can't touch it. Then I think, do you know what, I've had enough of the big corporate life anyway. So I decide that kind of role isn't for me.

'At around the same time I am starting to get approaches from some of the "elevator consultants." Three or four of the big American-based elevator consultants ask me if I am interested in joining them. They all have a common theme of opening up their business in Europe.

'I am, in fact, offered a job to take over one of the leading lift consultants in the UK. I have quiet some conversations about that too, but it comes to a point where I just think I've really had enough of

D2E. We are one for all and all for one. The squad here are on one of their many teambuilding days, this time climbing over the o2 which is much more enjoyable than the Ape in the Park event. Christmas gatherings include learning to do Bollywood dancing, the Gay Gordons in Edinburgh Castle and all the essential ingredients to keep employees' spirits high.

working for other people. It's clear that a lot of people seem to think that I can do consultancy, so I start talking with one or two people and ultimately I think, do you know what? I'm going to start my own consultancy.'So I start, with a firm over in the US, to see if I could work on a collaboration basis just to give myself full credibility as a consultant. That's the decision: I am going to go into consultancy.

'Then I get talking with a guy called Steve Truss who is at Otis and Steve is particularly keen to start a consultancy as well.

'I say to him: "Look, Steve, if you and I are going to start a consultancy we have to have some very robust guiding principles because I am not particularly impressed with the lift consultants that I've worked with in the UK. In contrast, I've worked with international elevator consultants in my time working in the US and they do work differently. Neither of them though, in my opinion, are doing a customer job, they are all doing "I am bigger than you" lift supplier stuff, "I know more about lifts than you do," that type of approach which is pure arrogance and I do not want to be doing that." 'So I say to Steve at the time: "The most important thing to me is that we actually have an organisation that has very high ethics. In fact," I say, "To me, one of the guiding principles of the company has to be ethics."

'In our industry, safety is a given, so that has to be another one. Then there's also a concern in my head about the quality of the end product being delivered in the UK because of my experience working over in Japan; I am seeing – at that time – a vast difference in the quality levels. So I say to him: "If you're interested in starting up a company, the company will be built around these pillars of safety, ethics and quality."

'Anyway I am then back in the States and meeting up with some old friends. We're out one early evening and I am telling them: "Look this is what I think I'm going to be doing, and one of the guys is a very good friend of mine from Otis, Dilip Rangnekar. 'So, anyway Dilip and I were out with a few people and he says: "So what are you going to do, Bill?" So I say: "Well I'm going to start a consultancy." He says: "Well how will that work? Because I don't really know how consultancy works." So I explain it all to him and I am using a napkin to write it down.

'So I say: "You start off with a design and then you work through the project, right the way through to execution of the project." He says: "Ah D2E!" So I look at him and I say: "Yeah that's a great name for the company. D2E, Design to Execution!"

'So that's how the name came about, but of course, having a consultancy that talks about "execution" in the UK is not such a good idea. So we say that D2E was really about Design to Elevation and that's how the name of the company comes about.

'The other thing is I am having a lot of thoughts about the nature of consultancy and consultants and what they are actually offering to their customers. To me, a consultant has only one "product" and that's their knowledge. So I say that our vision has to be about being the most knowledgeable in our field, because that's what the customer's buying.

'The customer's buying knowledge, information – but not necessarily experience. Although experience is important it can also be misconstrued as "when I," "when we," that type of approach. Knowledge is much more substantial than that. So the vision of the company is to be the most knowledgeable in our field and we start off firmly within that framework.

'Of course I then have to have all the stories behind safety, ethics and quality which will be the bedrock of the company. The way I see it is we might say we want to be the biggest and the best, but then so does everybody else. You will get the comment back: "Well, so what? What's the proof statement?"

'So when I look at the guiding principles, each of them has a story in the way that we talk to the people that are joining our company, the induction and the whole process.

So why is safety so important? 'In a way it speaks for itself, but we have an absolute obligation to make sure that all our employees go home safe at night. We have to have an obligation to make sure of that, and we can build onto this concept some different words today: their wellbeing is looked after. So the health and safety and the environment gets bigger by the day, and safety drives a lot of the culture of the company – in the way that we educate people on a continuous basis and how we measure ourselves on safety criteria.

'At the same time, we have an obligation to be designing lifts that are safe and to keep ensuring that we're giving the clients the right advice around codes and procedures and practices and so on.

'But then there's not so much written about ethics that you can use – or metrics in ethics for that matter. Ethics to me means that we're openly transparent about what we do. As a consultant you've got to make sure that you are truly independent and you are not compromised in any way.

'I really learned that when I worked in Singapore on the big new tube line extension on the MTR. I had to go to a meeting once a month at four o'clock on a Friday afternoon and everything that we said at that meeting was noted in the minutes and the minutes were shared publicly with all the potential suppliers.

'So there was never ever anything underhand or anything like that. You were being truly measured on your technical merit rather than from your back-channel dealings. Indeed, when it came to the submission of prices in Singapore they were all published on a notice board.

'I've been a victim of a consultant in my Otis days with a guy leading a Dutch auction behind my back. We subsequently lost a very big project because he was feeding information on to certain people.

'So I've said from the off, as far as ethics is concerned, we need to make sure that we're truly transparent, truly independent, with no compromise. We have rules around how we won't accept lunches, we won't go on factory visits, we won't indeed accept cups of tea but we will pay for everything and we will build a reputation that we will not be compromised in any shape or form. That has stood us in great stead right to this very day.

'Then, on the subject of quality, which is the final principle that the company has been built on, quality, again, I've experienced very different things in the three markets. You've got the Eastern Asian market, you've got the European market and then you've got, if you like, the US, or the Americas market.

'The quality expectation of those markets is so different. Working over in Japan particularly regarding the ride quality of lifts, the reliability of the lifts over there, is superior to what I've been used to in Europe and the US.

'The US have a market requirement, you know, to get the people there quickly, whereas in Asia it's to get the people there smoothly. 'So when we've started to talk about quality we've needed to put in place some tools in our specifications to say when you hand the lift over it's got to be 100% reliable. Again, when I worked in Singapore, their process, when they open up the tube line, is that for six months, the whole tube line from the entrances through to getting off the tube and coming out of the station is soft tested. So they prove their systems before they open it to the public. That type of concept did not exist in the lift industry.

'So what we've introduced is that the lifts must run for 48 hours before you can consider handing them over to the client, as opposed to when the provider has finished the lift: "Just sign here, and if they break down talk to the service department." We've built a set of tools around the quality as well. All of the guiding principles, the foundations for those guiding principles have to be built before we are ready to launch the company. To be honest, that takes a long time.

'What we also do is to understand what the market requirements are in the different segments and why would they want to use us, as opposed to using somebody else. So we have to have our value propositions built around the guiding principles.

'Then, back to the vision, where we say we want to be the most knowledgeable, we also say we would plough back profits into educating our employees so that they will grow their knowledge and, at the same time, add increasing value to our clients.

'We've got a fantastic record now of the number of people that have got Masters degrees through places like Northampton University. So we put our money where our mouth is rather than just have a bland, "Oh yeah, we want to be the most knowledgeable." Yeah, we do want to the be the most knowledgeable and this is what we do about it!

'It's a tremendous draw for people to want to come and work with us because that is our ethos and I have to say that that came about through what I learnt from George David at United Technologies, because, as we have learned in an earlier chapter, George was a big advocate of further education.

'The final thing behind building a company is to say well okay, what are your objectives of the company? We might have got guiding principles, but that's not an objective, we've got a vision, which is not an objective.

'Our objective... people say: "Well how big do you want to get, do you want to be the biggest and the best?" I say: "No, our objective is one thing only and that is customer satisfaction."

'For the focus of the company we will only have one metric of success, customer satisfaction. We will measure it on an annual basis. Believe it or not, for 16-17 years now we've used the same customer satisfaction survey template. We're able to measure improvements from one year to the next or indeed highlight degradation from one year to the next.

'At the same time, the information that we glean from our customer satisfaction is used to formulate our action plan for the forthcoming year. We also share the information with the employees so that they know what the customers are saying and this is what we have to work on. It's worked really, really well. So customer satisfaction is key.

'In the early days, because I've come from Otis, I am asked by some clients: "Are you actually an agent for Otis?" Of course I say: "Well, No, you go back to our guiding principles and you can see that I'm not an agent for Otis and we can never be that."

'Other people are saying: "So what are your objectives?" "Well," I say: "Customer satisfaction." They say: "Well, yeah, but that doesn't really mean anything to us, it means something to you." So

I say: "Look, you know we just want 10 customers and we just want to rock the socks off of those 10 customers and once we've got that we'll move onto the next objective."

'We don't want it to be anything numerically, we just want to work with some clients, make sure that we've got a good balance and really focus on customer satisfaction. It's worked well and we've now got a lot more than 10 customers, but we've scaled up from there.

'The other thing that I have learnt was that if you're going to grow the business you've got to walk the talk, and this is why it took so long for us to gear up in terms of sales because we needed to get in with the right clients and I've been absolutely adamant that we aren't going to work for anybody.

'This is back to Sandy Diehl and "You have to have a No." We've said: "No, we're not going to get involved in public tender work, we're not going to tender for it because if you're tendering for work you're always being judged just on your price."

'We've also said we wouldn't do any advertising. We would just work hard at trying to get a blue-chip client and we've said we wanted a blue-chip client in each of the sectors.

'I remember our small office, our first office after working from home. It is in Crawley and we have a whiteboard there and Robin Cheeseright writes up on the board, "Fosters." We walk into the office every day and see on the whiteboard, "Fosters."

'Why Fosters? Because Fosters is the number one architect in our minds and we say that's who we want to work with. We want to work with the best developer that we know at the time and that is Land Securities and we want to work with the best hotel group which is Hilton, and so on. Our goal is to work with blue-chip people because we want to be blue-chip ourselves. So the "No" worked.

'A couple of times we've slipped up. We get an opportunity to work for British Telecom, we get massively excited about that and are then told: "You do realise you've got to tender for this work and we think, well, we've gone down the road far enough with all of this, so we say: "Yeah, okay, and we work through Christmas

putting everything together. We put our price in and we are told:
"Sorry you've lost it – you're too expensive."

'We just think: well that just proves the point, there's no value
evaluation. "All that work you've done," they say, "That's interesting." But they are only really interested in the price.

'It proves the point that going into the public sector they're
so geared towards the cost that you're wasting your time and the
amount of money it costs you to put any bid together. So you have
to qualify out the work, and that's what we do now.

'So all of these things were the basis for building D2E and we
haven't changed track at all, we've kept completely on it.

'Yes, in recent years, we've added the guiding principle of sustainability, which is obviously important and the stories around that.
D2E is a real success story but in this story there's been some bumps.
I think the biggest bump of all is a classic case of "cash is king." 'It's
all very well making a load of profit and sending out invoices left,
right and centre, but unless they're getting paid you really can't take
your eye off the ball as an SME. People always say to you: "Cash is
king," and you say: "Yeah, yeah, you're right."

'But you don't realise just how important it is until one day
you've got no money in the bank and you've got to pay the salaries.
'That happens to me once. We are owed a lot of money and every
day I have to look into the bank account and see if the money has
come come in. It is now getting towards the end of the month
and I'm thinking: Oh Shit! I've got a problem here.'I go running
down to HSBC and say: "Can you help me because we're owed a
load of money, I've got to pay the salaries?" "Oh yeah," they say:
"You've been a good client, we'll help you out." I say: "Fine, I need
£25,000." They say: "Yeah, no problem. Just fill in these forms." So
I say: "So it's okay for me to pay the salaries this afternoon?" "Oh
no," they reply: "It'll take two weeks for it to get approved." So I
say… and remember I'm sitting in there, in the bank in Horsham, I
say: "I don't think you understand, I've got to pay these people today." They say: "Well, there's not a lot we can do. What we could
do is you could use an unauthorised overdraft facility up to £10,000,

whilst we're waiting for the £25,000, but we can't do much more."

'So what do I do? I have to pay it myself and I vow to myself I am never, ever going to have that awful nightmare again. When I say, nightmare, it was a nightmare because my pride wouldn't allow me to say to my staff: "I haven't got the money to pay you." I just couldn't live with myself.

'So I have to find the money to pay the people but after that I just thought I'm never, ever going to allow clients to put me into such a bad spot.

'The company was thriving, we were making profit but they weren't paying us and it's one of the things that I would say to any SME: make sure you're getting money up front. Make sure that you educate your clients on how you're going to run your business because you can have a great business and be in my situation and you haven't got the money to pay the salaries.

'Now fortunately, from a personal point of view, I am able to do that but I bet you a lot of SMEs don't have the reserves to do that. From that day on I have never, ever gone into the red.

'Sure enough, shortly afterwards, we do get paid and my focus is back hard on clients. The other thing I do when I start to grow the business is that I wouldn't employ sub-contractors or outsource any work.

'So, in a way I am creating a problem for myself in that all the employees are directly employed and so, in consequence, we are compelled to pay them on the 28th of the month or whatever it is, whereas if it is a sub-contractor you can play the game of pay when paid.

'So D2E has gone from zero up to a £4 million plus business. We employ 35 people today, we've got highly, highly qualified people within the company, we've got some really fantastic staff and their loyalty to the company is incredible.

'We've been through some tough times, Covid, the whole lot. We've looked after the staff 100% during Covid, we haven't reduced salaries or anything like that. I have supported 100% of everybody and we have just run the company on a family-orientation which a few people have criticised me for: "You're too paternal," they say. But I answer: "Well, yeah, I might be too paternal, but we've got a great company, we've got a great reputation and believe it or not, we make profit and we have a lot of money in the bank."

'After Steve Truss left, Robin Cheeseright came along. He'd been a guy that worked with me at Otis and left Otis under a redundancy programme, so he is able to fund himself for a period of time and I make it quite clear to him: "Robin I want you to come and work with me but I can't pay you" – which is quite interesting. So he looks at me and I say: "But what I will do, Robin, in exchange for you helping me rev up the company, I'll give you 10% of the business."

'I'm not going to give away anymore because the whole thing is mine, but I have to compensate Robin in some shape or form.

'He is being an utter gentleman, no two ways about it, and he says to me: "Well, surely, I should buy the 10%." I say: "No, I'm giving you 10% but I'm giving you 10% on the basis that one day we'll start earning money." Which is what happens. Then many years later he decides that he wants to retire from consultancy and do some private stuff, so I pay him out a considerable amount of money. So his 10% ends up being a great investment.

'Looking forward, is an interesting subject for any SME who starts up a business that becomes successful because the founder may want to retire or come out of it or whatever.

'It's like getting married; you have children and then one horrible day they decide they're going to leave home and you think, Oh My God, my life's empty, the house is too big, there's no noise. It's an important point behind the D2E name in that restaurant conversation with Dilip in Hartford, Connecticut.

'The name coincides with how the company works. One of the things I say to Dilip back then is that I definitely don't want to call the business "Bill Evans Consultancy" because there's no longevity to it. I remember all the competitors in the UK at the time are named after the principal, so, when the principal retires, it's as if the company has folded.

'When I start D2E I deliberately do not want to have any name associated with it for longevity reasons.

'So here we are today, 20 years later, and the company's well-established and well-known as D2E. There's no reason at all why it can't continue in its current form, with a structure that doesn't rely on me dealing with the day-to-day stuff.

'We have a wonderful team led by managing director, Mark Fair-weather and director, Martin Fuller, associate directors, Paul Burns and Rony Eappen, and many other fantastic associates such as Amy Dacres-Dixon . Apart from making sure that we stick to the straight and narrow, ie our own guiding principles, what we are doing with customers is just keeping on going down the same track.

'The company can carry on for a long, long period of time with or without me, because the family own the business, as part of our family foundation. In fact, I really believe in the family orientation.

If, however, there was an organisation with a similar ethos out there which wanted to buy D2E (and I'm pretty sure they'd be few and far between), who wanted to collaborate, and there was going to be a genuine benefit to do that, then I or the family foundation would consider that. But meanwhile, the family own D2E.

'My daughter, Emily is a director of the company and she, alongside my son, George, who is a shareholder, is there to safeguard the family investment. She knows the lift industry, she is well versed in relevant technologies and holds a Masters degree, an MBA.

'I think looking forward is one of the most important things any company can do, and this is advice given to me by one of the guys at Land Securities many years ago. He would say: "D2E are a great company, you do a really good job for us and we value you highly, but don't get complacent."

'Complacency: you can fall into the trap by thinking: "We've arrived." But the reality is the marketplace is constantly changing. If you use one of the tools that we've spoken about earlier in the book, PEST analysis, to review the political, economic, social and technology trends, you'll soon see what's going on today. Everyone's talking about digitalisation, artificial intelligence, all those sorts of things.

'Is there a possibility that somebody will come up with some machine that does away with the lift consultant altogether? Maybe. You have to move with the times and one of the most important things about you moving with the times is that you must move fast. You can't drag your feet because if you do, someone will be there before you and then you're on catchup.

'So yeah, it's important for a consultancy to be the most knowledgeable, and part of that knowledge is actually to know what's out there in the future.

'Currently we're continuing our deep study of IOT, Internet of Things, and one of our lads, Paul Clements, who has just got his chartership has just been presenting that subject on the worldwide stage.

'So, I've said to him: "Paul, great, but what's next? You've got to keep on pushing, what's next?"

'Now we're in this digital age where we work in an environment where technology is a fundamental requirement; we've got to know all about artificial intelligence, digitalisation, robotics, all of those sort of things.

'You never arrive, you've got to keep pushing.'

You can build a company in the way YOU want. Don't compromise your vision when others tell you how to price or how to run things.

• • •

Don't be too influenced by what competitors do, don't do advertising if your vision is to not do it… Have the best intentions and then keep your focus on your high standards!

• • •

When starting a new company, get clear on a couple of things before you start. Having the foundations right pays off in the long run.

See the bigger picture, how you fit in, and why you are different. Why would clients pick you instead of competition?

• • •

Your guiding principles, the stories behind them, and the proof that you walk the talk are vital.

• • •

Have a clear set of rules around the practical application of your company's values, so it's easy for everyone to stick to it, and you automatically build a reputation.

Set out your objective. How will you measure
success and build action plans around:

•

The core of your product and how you'll make
sure this is the best in the market?

•

The type of clients and projects you say
'Yes' or 'No' to?

•

Your ideal clients and collaborators?

This will keep everyone motivated toward the
same vision, and will provide a clear guideline
when you come to face a dilemma.

Think deeply about your pricing strategy, and how and when you expect clients to pay you so you can grow your business solidly for everyone who depends on you.

• • •

Make yourself replaceable, so the company can continue working and growing without you.

• • •

Keep looking forward, keep pushing. You have never arrived. Never get complacent.

Published in 2024 by
UK Book Publishing

ukbookpublishing.com
First floor, Unit 5
305 Whitley Road
Whitley Bay
Tyne and Wear
NE26 2HU

ISBN 978 1 916572 55 3

Designed by Prof. Phil Cleaver &
Jenny Penny of et al design consultants.
Typeset in Bembo Arcadian.

Printed in Great Britain
by Amazon

44002294R00116